NO MORE COTTON CANDY

Jim Hennesy

Energizing
Your Spiritual Life with More of
God's Presence and Power

NO MORE COTTON CANDY

FOREWORD BY
CINDY JACOBS

NO MORE COTTON CANDY

Energizing Your Spiritual Life with More of
God's Presence and Power

Jim Hennesy

www.onwardbooks.com

Book Design by Aleksandr Novik, Novik Design

Printed in the United States of America
ISBN: 1-880689-28-6

CONTENTS

DEDICATION

This simple work represents my inordinate passion for the church. Viewing myself as a stakeholder in Christ's church, I've contended for her effectiveness and endeavored to press out the margins of her current definitions and influences. Origins for passion and vision can be clearly traced to all my families. For that reason, I dedicate this book to:

Dr. James and Margie Hennesy, my parents, who cultivated my appetite for spiritual things by displaying genuine testimony of Jesus. They developed my dissatisfaction with institutional religion.

To Becky, Ross, Ryan and Katee Hennesy. My wife and children relentlessly deliver God's grace. They are my greatest earthly treasures.

And to my Trinity Church family, the most courageous and resolved Christians I know. The journey we are taking together provides the adventure of a lifetime.

FOREWORD BY CINDY JACOBS

Seven years ago my husband and I made a move back to our roots in Texas. As we have a deep conviction that every traveling ministry needs a good local church and a pastor to watch after our souls, we went searching for that often illusive mixture—a spiritual family and a shepherd.

Mike and I walked into Trinity Church and sat down. Both of us felt a bit uncomfortable in the new setting. Yet at the same time we were carefully listening to the still small voice inside of us. We heard a whisper, *You're home.*

Pastor Jim Hennesy stood up to preach and I instantly knew he was a shepherd who loved his sheep. As he preached I could hear his heart's cry to live authentic Christianity—the deep kind of faith that is the same on Monday through Saturday as it is on Sunday. I could tell from his message that he had been through some pretty deep waters, yet he retained his passion for his people and his love for God.

Later I heard the story of how he had come to Cedar Hill, Texas, a city just south of Dallas, answering the call to what some would consider a pastor's graveyard.

He took a church that had been devastated by a former leader who was charismatic but seriously flawed morally.

As time went on, Jim Hennesy agreed to be our shepherd. This was no easy job, I might say! From that time he has stood with us in our distresses, cried with us in times of sorrow, prayed for and supported us. His wife, Becky (Beck to the Trinity family), has become my dear friend.

We have seen this man fast, lead prayer, hold babies in his arms and shed compassionate tears when their little bodies were eaten up with disease. He is a shepherd after God's own heart. So, who better to write this book, which is so aptly titled *No More Cotton Candy*? Only someone who is convinced that too much sugar can give a person "spiritual diabetes." Jim is full of passion for Jesus and he desires to transform his city.

He has the passion to eradicate systemic poverty as well as care for the plight of the single mothers and dads who have lost their jobs. He has a belief in the Holy Spirit's power to see healing, and yet he doesn't lose faith in God when one of the members of his congregation receives the ultimate healing of heaven rather than the one he cried for on earth.

As we study the history of the local churches in America, and many other nations for that matter, we see them as bastions of righteousness fighting the moral ills of society. Jim Hennesy makes a strong case that sugar-coated messages only lead to societal decay both on the personal and corporate levels. When the church understands that we are called to be the passionate, purposeful, prayerful body that Jim writes about in this book, we will become the moral and spiritual backbone of our nation once again.

Alex de Tocqueville was said to have written these words: "Not until I went into the churches of America and heard her pulpits flame with righteousness did I understand the secret of her genius and power. America is great because she is good. And if America ever ceases to be good, she will cease to be great."

I believe it is possible that we can see our nation change because of our intimate relationship with God. But Jim Hennesy says we must give up our spiritual addiction to life without substance so that we can achieve our spiritual destiny.

If you know life can be more than one big roller coaster ride of spiritual highs and lows, this book is for you. If you have said to your friend, husband or wife, "There just has to be more to Christianity than what I'm experiencing," then open these pages and read each chapter. This book is like a roadmap to an abundant life. I guarantee you won't be disappointed!

Cindy Jacobs
Founder Generals International
Red Oak, Texas

ENDORSEMENTS

No More Cotton Candy challenges believers to go beyond religious ritual so they can experience more of the Spirit's guidance and power. Pastor Jim Hennesy's personal journey and spiritual insights will fill readers with anticipation for the miraculous in their own lives.

George O. Wood
General Superintendent
General Council of the Assemblies of God

○ ○ ○

The first time I read *No More Cotton Candy* I cried with conviction and invited God to do a fresh work in my life. Author Jim Hennesy looks readers in the eye and says it like it is.

Hal Donaldson
Founder and President
Convoy of Hope

° ° °

Having seen the fruits of Trinity Church in Cedar Hill under the pastoral leadership of Jim Hennesy, it is clear that God's Holy Spirit is in control all the time. Just like the Christ-centered twelve steps of recovery program lead a person from empty addictions to a spiritual awakening, *No More Cotton Candy* leads us from sweet, fluffy religion to spiritual purpose in the body of Christ that is His Church.

I dearly enjoyed this book. It is appropriate for group study using the probing questions Jim has penned. Pastor Hennesy has such inspired insight into God's purpose for His people.

Rob Franke, Mayor
Cedar Hill, Texas

° ° °

No More Cotton Candy boldly addresses the spiritual condition of American Christianity. Many churchgoers have been standing in line for sweet, sugary, spinning stuff that dissolves upon touch or taste. This book confronts traditional Sunday-morning spirituality by offering a vision for how the life of Jesus impacts daily opportunities and routines. It particularly helps people discover new metaphors to re-image their spiritual lives away from institutionalism. Essentially, this book is an invitation to a spiritual journey that celebrates the mystery of knowing Jesus while illustrating the day-to-day attainment of the life Jesus offers.

Jim Hennesy writes about real life. He effectively presents an image of a local Church and its pastor facing struggles and setbacks yet finding solutions, grace and favor in the community. New Testament theology, especially regarding the kingdom of God and its supernatural components, is embedded in entertaining anecdotes and easy applications. *No More Cotton Candy* begins each chapter with a life-giving, kingdom principle in non-religious language and concludes with penetrating questions for personal or group discussion.

No More Cotton Candy is an answer to prayer. Anyone who has longed to see the Church recapture its destiny as the great hope of the world will find a true spiritual soul mate in Pastor Jim Hennesy. I found his honest and open personal journey into the heart of God to be filled with encouragement and practicality. I have seen Trinity Church experience authentic spiritual transformation and become an international voice for genuine Christian community and renewal. If your heart longs to see the Church rise again into its God-given destiny, this is the book for you.

Randal Ross, Pastor
Calvary Church
Naperville, Illinois

INTRODUCTION

The setting was almost perfect. White sand caressed our toes, ocean waves lathered our feet and a warm sun tanned our shoulders. Like newlyweds on a honeymoon, my wife, Beck, and I walked hand-in-hand along a picturesque Florida beach. Beyond the serenity, however, was the painful reality that we would soon be returning to our home in Cedar Hill, Texas, to face the "soap opera" in our local church.

A painful reality crashed over this moment like waves over a sandcastle. Suddenly, as if a thunderstorm had moved in and shielded the sun's rays, Beck had lost hope. Through clenched teeth she told me: "Jim, you can go back to that church if you want, but I'm never going back! They don't like me and I don't like them. It's over."

Now, that's a real problem when your wife of nineteen years says she won't attend the church where you serve as senior pastor.

"Beck, I love you," I said. "Just tell me what you want me to do. I'll sell cars. I'll write insurance. I'll even enter the World Series of Poker!" I tried to lighten her mood, but she wasn't buying it.

"What I want," she said without emotion, "is to start walking into that ocean and never come back."

The tone of her voice let me know me she was serious. She wanted out of the ministry. She was weary of attending church services that lacked God's presence and power. She was tired of seeing Christians raise their hands in worship on Sunday and wave their fists in anger at one another during the week. In her mind, attending church was no longer just a weekly obligation; it had become a prison sentence.

"Jim," she said firmly, "things have to change. I don't believe this is what Christ intended for the church. And it's not what He wants for us. Spiritually, we need something more."

I had to admit Beck was right. We had become addicted to what I call "cotton candy"—a sweet-tasting brand of religion that offers a quick emotional fix but little spiritual value. My father was a great pastor, so I had grown up in church. I knew how to officiate a church service, but for years God's presence had been lacking. I knew the form but had lost the power. I had relied more on my natural ability than the leading of the Holy Spirit.

It was apparent God was calling Beck and me, and our congregation, to a new place of wholeness and spiritual authority. No longer could we settle for less than God's best. Somehow I knew there were others in our church who felt the same way; they just didn't know how to break the cotton candy addiction. We were stuck in a serious spiritual rut.

"Honey," I said, "if we go back and give it another try, I know things are going to change. We're going to change."

Beck didn't respond immediately. She continued to stare at the ocean as the waves washed the shoreline. She was measuring the level of conviction in my words.

"Jim, I don't think I can play church anymore," she said. "I'm tired of going through the motions."

Beck's raw honesty and desperate concerns became the tipping point for the greatest adventure of our lives. At that moment we had no tangible reason to expect things would improve. Yet we had little choice but to keep moving forward. "Let's give it one more chance," I begged. "Let's give God a chance."

She took a deep breath before nodding. "Okay, one more chance."

Tears surfaced in her eyes and I took her in my arms. I tried to convince her things would get better but she and I both knew my words were more wishful than anything. I listened to the pounding of the surf in the background. I wanted to believe my own words, but I knew we were drowning in a sea of religion. Only God himself could toss us the right life preserver.

That moment proved to be a critical turnaround for us. As we cried out to God for answers and invited Him to take control of our seemingly hopeless situation, the Holy Spirit began to move in a fresh way in our lives and in our congregation: I began to speak with greater authority, and, week after week, the altars were filled with people repenting of sin and seeking healing. Longstanding conflicts were resolved. The Church began to grow in numbers as well as in spiritual depth.

Today—sixteen years after that pivotal moment on the beach—Trinity Church is alive, unified, compassionate and generous. The Church that once appeared to be suffocating under the weight of religion has found new life and become a force for God in the community of Cedar Hill—and beyond.

The crisis of faith that Beck and I experienced on that beach in Florida is more common than anyone cares to admit. How many times have we heard people say they'll never set foot in a church again because of hypocrisy, legalism and manipulative pleas for money? How many Christians who once served faithfully in a local congregation are now boycotting church altogether because they became disappointed and disillusioned? How many have vowed to never return because they believe church leaders are selfish, egotistical or even immoral?

Hopefully, when we hear those indictments, we feel the sting of their words—because they're talking about us. We are the Church. People are looking for something real—something that goes beyond empty rituals or Sunday morning theatrics. They want to see the words of Jesus lived out in His people. They want authenticity. They're looking for genuine relationships with sincere people who are full of God's love.

This book isn't a rant against the Church. It is an acknowledgement of the Church's failures and a call to all of us to pursue a dynamic Christian life. If believers are spiritually healthy and Church leaders are focused, the Church will be both relevant and life-giving. It is not time to write the Church's obituary; rather, it's time to invite the Holy Spirit to ignite the spiritual lives of all believers so that local Churches can come alive.

Unfortunately some Christians are content to live on cotton candy religion. Cotton candy is pure sugar—all fluff and spin—and the sticky stuff dissolves almost instantly in your mouth. Nevertheless people line up all day at carnivals and fairs for their sweet fix.

Perhaps that describes some believers today: they're addicted to a form of Christianity that offers temporary relief through empty promises but, ultimately, delivers nothing of real substance. Much of the so-called Christian message today is filled with these fluffy, sugary promises—whether they are preached from our glittering pulpits, showcased on Christian television or radio or published in best-selling books. Many American preachers focus their message on prosperity and promises of selfish gain while their followers are struggling in their relationships with God and others. We offer Band-aids when people need serious heart surgery. And believers continue to come back for heaping portions of what amounts to nothing—even if it leaves them unfulfilled.

In times of frustration, when I felt like abandoning my calling as a Christian leader, I had to remind myself that the church is the vehicle God created to provide us with substantive help that can't be found anywhere else. The church is God's plan, and there is no Plan B. That is why it is so destructive when the church sells sugar rather than the meat of God's Word. People become satisfied with less than God's best for their lives. They also enter Sunday church services oblivious to His presence and ambivalent toward His supernatural power. They fail to experience the love, joy, compassion and life of a church that functions under the headship of Jesus Christ and in the power of the Holy Spirit. So, in essence, they don't even know what they're missing.

No More Cotton Candy is intended to whet your appetite for more of God's reality and give you a vision for a more fulfilling life and church experience. It will challenge you to break out of the religious bubble. This book also provides a portrait of practical spirituality—an empowering faith that guides your actions, thoughts, attitudes and speech throughout the week. These pages provide a road map to wholeness for those who need healing and reconciliation.

If you are one of the millions who are weary of playing church and going through the motions, be assured that God longs to replace an addiction to cotton candy with a healthy hunger for His power and presence. He can do it for you. He can do it for your local church. My sincere prayer is that He will do it for all of us.

> *Why do we allow new realities and changing circumstances to steal our dreams for a more fulfilling, spiritually energized life?*

THE LIFE YOU WANT

My Little League coach just didn't like me. Well, at least he didn't like my game. With one command, he dashed my hopes of playing professional baseball. He told me: "Young fellah, take a seat on the bench."

A few years later, my dreams of becoming an astronaut also faded when I discovered sixth-grade math was a requirement for flying space shuttles. And my aspirations to be the lead singer for the rock band Chicago died when I was booted from the church choir!

Needless to say, I learned at an early age that sometimes dreams have to be replaced by new realities.

A freshman in college, for example, might say confidently to himself, *I'm going to fall in love, pass the bar exam, buy a big house, earn lots of money and serve as block captain for my neighborhood watch.* But four years later, when he ends up with a broken heart, bad grades and no serious job offers, he may have a change of plans. At that point he might say to himself, *I think I'll find a different girl, change my career path, find a job that can pay my rent—and I'll buy a watchdog.* Our dreams tend to change when we are confronted with tough circumstances.

However, God's dreams for our lives never change. Jeremiah 29:11 (NIV) says: "'For I know the plans I have for you,' declares the Lord, 'plans to prosper you and not to harm you, plans to give you hope and a future.'" Why do we settle for less than God's best when we have this promise? Why do we allow new realities and changing circumstances to steal our dreams for a more fulfilling, spiritually energized life?

In John 10:10 (NKJV), Jesus said He came so we might have life "more abundantly." He did not say, "I came that you might survive." He didn't die on the cross so we could have a mediocre existence. He promised abundance and fulfillment! Every follower of Jesus has reason to anticipate a life of peace, joy, purpose and adventure. Anything less falls short of God's will for our lives.

Fortunately, access to God's promises is not dependent on our ability to hit a Major League curve ball, pass a sixth-grade math test, or pass the bar exam or secure a six-figure salary. As followers of Jesus, we simply have to express our desire for more of His power and presence, and be willing to do whatever is necessary to see God's dreams for our lives come to fruition.

All of us need gasoline to power our cars and fuel to heat our homes. Yet in today's world we are constantly reminded that there is an energy crisis. One explosion on an oil tanker in the Gulf of Mexico or one military conflict in the Middle East is enough to send the price of oil skyrocketing.

Yet there is no energy crisis in the spiritual realm. God has an endless supply of His Spirit's power for His people. We can call this renewable energy or unlimited power. That is what Jesus offers us. He promises to convey His love and power through us if we love Him for who He is rather than for what He provides. In other words, loving Jesus fully results in unlimited power and abundant living.

LAUGHING AT ADVERSITY

I learned this lesson long ago when our family faced a serious health crisis. My wife announced one day, through tears, that her mother had been diagnosed with Alzheimer's disease. I tried to offer comfort with assurances of God's love and healing power. But Beck and I both knew this could be the beginning of an arduous journey for our family.

Twelve years passed. Despite prayers and medication, Alzheimer's continued to steal memories from Beck's mom. Then we received word that doctors didn't expect her to survive the night.

The family converged from around the country to stand around Mom's bed and say goodbye to a great woman of faith. For four sleepless nights, while awaiting her final breath, we exchanged stories about Mom and thanked God for her influence in our lives. The stage was set for her to peacefully enter the gates of heaven.

Yet, surprisingly, that final breath never came. Mom had a resurgence of vitality. As the bedside vigil came to an end, and family members made plans to return to their respective homes, we all retreated to a nearby restaurant. We were weary and perhaps confused by the turn of events, but laughter became our medicine that night.

What began with giggles soon became belly laughter that could be heard throughout the restaurant. (I'm sure patrons assumed we were drunk!) Finally, the manager paid us a visit to see what we were celebrating. No one was about to tell him that Mom's impending death had brought us together.

As this "party" continued, I tried to analyze the moment. Amid our grief there was remarkable joy. No one had spiked our drinks. Were we simply in serious psychological denial? No, Jesus was paying us a visit. He was with us. He offered us a virtual feast of joy. I could almost see Him sitting at our table ordering onion rings and drinking iced tea with us.

Why am I so surprised by His presence? I asked myself. Later, more questions filled my mind: *What if God intends the difficulties of life to push us into deeper treasures? What if current problems lead to eternal splendor? What if suffering results in glory? What if problems designed to get us down actually lift us up? Don't we want a relationship with a loving God who helps us in our time of trouble and ensures that all things work together for good?*

The answers to my questions led to one profound conclusion: I wanted a life where joy and laughter weren't eroded by difficult circumstances. I wanted to know God's overcoming power.

Conversely, I imagined how life, for many people, is a series of defeats and disappointments with no hope of escape or eternal life. What they assume they can rely on for strength in times of trouble—marriages, jobs, money, friendships, fame, talents, low credit card interest rates, and good health care coverage—actually crumbles under the pressures of reality.

Let's face it: A life without pain does not exist. Everyone experiences grief and disappointment. But as we pass through life's hardships we face a choice. Will we try to face tough times alone? Or will we invite Jesus to sit at our table to give us strength, courage and laughter? Jesus invites us to take the second option. He said in Matthew 11:28: "Come to Me, all who are weary and heavy-laden, and I will give you rest."

FOLDING TOWELS

Our perspective on life is shaped by what we're taught by our parents, grandparents, siblings, neighbors and friends. Right or wrong, their tastes and values rub off on us. Shortly after Beck and I were married, believe it or not, our first argument was about how towels should be folded. I insisted on a tri-fold and Beck preferred a ridiculous, less efficient square-fold! Our towel-folding feuds became quite intense.

When we finally called a truce, we realized our arguments could be traced back to our upbringing. Beck had been taught to fold towels differently than people in the Hennesy clan had taught me. I thought that if I acquiesced to a square-folded towel, it was an admission of an inferior upbringing. Finally we resolved the issue by agreeing to keep two sets of towels.

Fortunately we've matured a little since then. Our debates have moved on from towels to more complicated issues—like restaurant preferences! But our childish disagreements illustrate how people tend to stake out their allegiances and remain loyal to them, even when they're wrong.

In high school, my baseball hero was Brooks Robinson of the Baltimore Orioles. So, I ate the cereal with his face on the box, shaved with the razor he advertised and chewed the bubble gum he endorsed. It's no different today. Many people look up to celebrities such as Oprah Winfrey, Jay Leno, Brad Pitt, Martha Stewart or Tom Cruise. Driven by envy, they anoint these famous people to be their personal gurus. They look at them and think, *If I could be like them, I would have the kind of life I want.*

Why are people more inclined to follow the teachings of a celebrity than they are to adhere to the principles espoused by Jesus Christ? They spend more time reading self-help authors than seeking the Savior, who actually possesses the power to give them a better life. He calls His brand of life "abundant," "overcoming" and "eternal." Meanwhile, today's gurus get rich selling books and DVDs that, at best, offer deceptive results.

The life Jesus offers is not one that promises major league championships or Hollywood blockbusters. In fact, He doesn't guarantee material wealth, fame, perfect health, weight loss or marriage bliss. Instead, what He offers is counterintuitive. It involves turning the other cheek, going the extra mile, forgiving one's enemies and serving others. Jesus instructs us to follow Him and His principles and, in turn, He offers to give us a life we never dreamed was possible.

MORE THAN BASEBALL

As a teen, I assumed if I could just play baseball as well as Brooks Robinson I'd enjoy life at its highest level. Unfortunately I didn't have his fielding range, arm strength or bat speed. I finally concluded I didn't need Brooks to imitate; I needed him to indwell me. But I was never going to be Brooks Robinson, and there was no way he was going to enter my soul. I had no chance at becoming a star on the baseball diamond.

Fortunately, somewhere along the way, I learned there was more to life than baseball, personal achievement and athletic trophies. Perhaps by observing my parents' generosity, I discovered that giving to others brought more fulfillment than serving myself.

Some Christians claim that performing good deeds leads to a more fulfilling life, but their words are hollow because the life they promote is not the life they live. They've settled for a poor imitation of Jesus instead of the indwelling Jesus. In reality, they tend to be more preoccupied with their careers and personal comfort than they are the needs of others.

Every week people enter our church in Texas seeking help: a husband whose wife cheated on him; a daughter who was caught using drugs; a worker who lost his job;

a mother who discovered she has cancer. They come to us afraid, depressed, heartbroken, lonely, and at times even suicidal. They come seeking hope in a place where they think Jesus might be present. They come seeking help from people who are indwelled with the compassion of Christ. We have the privilege of drying their tears, healing their hurts and introducing them to Jesus. What they may not know is that we are finding fulfillment by investing in their lives.

You will never discover this abundant life if you focus your life on your own needs. You must fight to overcome the stronghold of selfishness. I learned this a few years ago, when I realized that my belt size had increased six inches since I had been in college. I immediately began an exercise routine.

Finally, after many hours in the gym, I was able to buy smaller pants. But a conflict remained between my new affinity for fitness and my love of pecan pie. Needless to say, it remains important to my waistline that fitness wins the battle.

Likewise, a battle is being waged to determine what we will love most. The enemy of our soul wants us to love the wrong things. In Philippians 1:9, Paul prays that his friends would experience a journey where "love may abound still more and more in real knowledge and all discernment, so that you may approve the things that are excellent." The apostle explains that life's choices are determined by what we love. Most of us spend our lives on things unworthy of life's potential. But our lives flourish when we make decisions based on what Jesus loves.

What does Jesus love? He loves people, of course. And He wants us to love them as much as we love ourselves.

The television game show *Who Wants To Be a Millionaire* is brilliantly produced. Lights and music are timed perfectly to build suspense for every question. Each contestant is given an opportunity to answer questions that could ultimately yield a million-dollar payoff. Along the way, contestants are given three "lifelines." They can ask the audience, eliminate some choices or phone a friend.

We've often seen people phone a friend when they needed an answer to win $1 million on this program. Yet there are many people who refuse to call upon Jesus Christ, the greatest Friend of all, when they face a serious life challenge.

What if you were diagnosed with cancer? What if your son or daughter were addicted to drugs? What if your spouse had cheated on you? Wouldn't you use a lifeline to call a Friend who has the answers you need? Jesus has the answers, and we can call Him anytime and anywhere. He also wants His followers to volunteer to be lifelines for others in need. If, for example, Jesus has helped you overcome depression, loneliness, alcoholism, abuse or betrayal, you are more than qualified to take a call from someone who has faced these problems. Jesus wants to use your testimony to impart strength and hope to someone else.

The extraordinary life we seek is "others-oriented." Along my spiritual journey I've encountered remarkable people who have found fulfillment by being a lifeline to others. For example, Alan, a city manager, has helped our community move from an obscure, economically challenged city into a dynamic culture of enterprise and prosperity. He declared publicly that the city would follow the principles of Jesus, and he openly prayed for business leaders, school principals, firefighters and police officers. He enlisted city leaders to support a clear vision of hope and love. He imparts strength to his city because he receives strength from another world.

Another example is Sheila. Given her failed marriages, her life story could have been the basis for a depressing movie on the Lifetime Network. Fortunately her story has a happy ending because she found real life in Jesus. For years, the corporate world was her priority, but Jesus reordered her decisions and focus. Today she is a lifeline to many emotionally wounded people.

Bruce and Camella also serve Jesus by serving others. Unable to have children of their own, they leveraged their circumstance to launch a business that exists to help children around the world. Their lives are fulfilling because they dedicated themselves to being lifelines to homeless children.

Take a minute to evaluate how you are spending your life. Is it the life you always wanted? Are your goals focused on yourself? Or are you living to help others? More importantly, are you living the abundant life God promised you?

QUESTIONS FOR DISCUSSION:

1. *When you were younger, what were your life ambitions? What kind of life do you want now?*
2. *What do you think Jesus meant when He said He would give us an abundant life?*
3. *What changes must occur in your life to become less focused on self?*

> *For many, their salvation is limited to the forgiveness of sin and a guarantee of heaven. They've embraced heaven's streets of gold without receiving Christ's promise of power on Earth.*

UNDER THE INFLUENCE

A century ago, Germantown, Pennsylvania (a suburb of Philadelphia), was known for its magnificent mansions, immaculate streets and expansive factories. Yet today the buildings are dilapidated and the streets are laden with graffiti and broken down automobiles. Without leaving your car, you can smell poverty, crime and drugs. Many of Germantown's citizens reside there because hope has eluded them. But this is where my son,

Ross, and his wife, Angela, decided to relocate after they graduated from college. They could have moved to a cleaner, safer, more prosperous suburban community; instead they chose to live among a people they were called to serve by developing urban farms and drug rehabilitation programs.

The contrast between Ross' world and mine is stark. Cedar Hill, Texas, is a growing bedroom community near Dallas with chic shopping plazas, nice restaurants and a low crime rate. But one Sunday afternoon I found myself in a gang-infested part of the city. I suddenly wished I had a few tattoos and more "street-cred," because I could feel I was not welcome there. If the looks of residents could kill, I was already dead.

The irony of it all was striking: Hours earlier, our church in the tidy suburbs had celebrated God's presence and experienced the miraculous. But just a few miles away there were no such signs of God's power. All I could see were dilapidated businesses and hopeless people, just like I'd witnessed in Germantown.

The apostle Paul may have encountered similar hopelessness and despair when he came to the ancient port city of Ephesus. But it was in that place that he wrote these words in Ephesians 3:14 (The Message): "My response is to get down on my knees before the Father … I ask Him that … you'll be able to take in with all followers of Jesus the extravagant dimensions of Christ's love."

Paul may have fallen to his knees after seeing so many wounded and empty people. But he also bowed before Almighty God because he could envision a church that possessed the potential to offer real help and hope to places like Germantown and Dallas. He was persuaded that the miserable condition of cities like Ephesus did not have to dictate their future condition. He believed in God's power to restore and transform lives, churches and communities. He believed God longed to release a new influence on the Earth.

KNOCKED OFF HIS HORSE

Paul's salvation experience gave him credentials to pronounce hope in any situation. Once an enemy of Christ and His followers, Paul experienced God's transformational power while riding his horse to the city of Damascus. After being knocked from his saddle and temporarily blinded, Paul never saw the Church the same way again. He viewed the Church as more than a museum for institutional religion. He saw it as Christ's holy bride, the temple of the Holy Spirit and the steward of hope to lost people and communities in need. He saw an empowered Church that was fully under the influence of the Holy Spirit.

Paul wrote to the Ephesians: "God can do anything, you know—far more than you could ever imagine or guess or request in your wildest dreams! He does it not by pushing us around but by working within us, his Spirit deeply and gently within us. Glory to God in the church! Glory to God in the Messiah, in Jesus! Glory down all the generations! Glory through all millennia! Oh, yes!" (Ephesians 3:20, The Message). He also told them how he would pray for them:

"I ask—ask the God of our Master, Jesus Christ, the God of glory—to make you intelligent and discerning in knowing him personally, your eyes focused and clear, so that you can see exactly what it is he is calling you to do, grasp the immensity of this glorious way of life he has for his followers, oh, the utter extravagance of his work in us who trust him—endless energy, boundless strength!" (Ephesians 1:18,19, The Message).

Paul also told the Ephesian Christians that Christ had been raised from the dead, and that they had been seated with Him "in the heavenly places far above all principality and power and might and dominion ... And He put all things under His feet" (Ephesians 1:20-22, NKJV).

Paul's vision for Christ's followers had them in a new position: Seated at the right hand of God, tapping into resurrection strength, revealing deeply hidden mysteries and treasures, and living far above life's traps and tribulations. Yet, many believers today contradict Paul's description. They are not living above their circumstances. They're too busy rushing to work, tending to kids, shopping for groceries, yelling at traffic and paying their bills. The last time they talked about "exceeding great power" they were referring to the Dallas Cowboys' new stadium, with its retractable roof and massive digital replay board.

What are we missing? The kind of dramatic salvation that Paul experienced on the road to Damascus led to a life of power, under the influence of the Holy Spirit. Yet for many Christians today, salvation is limited to the forgiveness of sins and a guarantee of heaven. Conversion is merely a form of "fire insurance" so they don't have to go to hell. They've embraced heaven's streets of gold without receiving Christ's promise of power on earth.

WHAT HAPPENED TO SUNDAY MORNINGS?

On Sundays, rather than the typical nod-and-yawn church service, believers need to be left speechless by the wonders and miracles of God. We need our breath taken away as we behold His glory. Perhaps we need fewer explanations and more demonstrations of His power. This would transform our outlook on life and bring hope to people and places that are crumbling before our eyes.

Jesus wants to flabbergast the Earth with manifestations of His grace. Throughout His ministry, He seized opportunities to demonstrate His love and power. In Luke 5, Jesus captured Peter's attention by instructing him to lower his nets in deep water at midday. No doubt Peter rolled his eyes, saying to himself, *Jesus, you make a great religious leader, but leave the fishing to me. Everyone knows you don't fish during the day and certainly not in deep water.*

Peter complied with Jesus' request just to prove his point. Yet Jesus made His point by overflowing Peter's nets to the extent they were breaking. There were so many fish that the boat almost capsized! Peter witnessed a demonstration of Christ's power and, instantly, his perspective and priorities changed.

In the middle of the fishing frenzy, Peter turned to Jesus and said, "Leave! Depart!" Why would Peter decline the help of the world's greatest fisherman when, at this rate, he could have opened a string of Long John Silver franchises? Peter feared experiencing too much of God's power. He knew if Jesus could see fish below the water's surface, He could see the sin in his heart.

Peter rightly assumed there was more power where this miracle came from. Jesus had taken his breath away.

The Man he had designated as a good teacher and religious leader was much more than that; He was indeed the Son of God. It was Peter's moment of realization that his image of Jesus was too small, and he was afraid of what this could mean.

Fear is, in part, the reason places like Germantown, Pennsylvania, are dying without hope. Some believers—and for that matter, entire congregations—are afraid to invite God to manifest His power in their lives and cities. They want just enough of God to be personally secure, but not enough to transform a desperate world. In other words, they prefer a Sunday morning yawn to the discomfort that comes when God convicts them of sin and takes their breath away.

Jesus saw the fear in Peter's eyes. He said to him, in essence, *I see you to the core. I see your sin. But I won't leave you. I've come to show you how to live with the Father's presence and power.*

The same Jesus who filled Peter's nets also knows the intricacies of business, health, education, politics, relationships, and church, and how to bring hope to broken cities and desperate people. He is just looking for people through whom He can work. He is searching for people who live under His full influence.

A church qualifies to offer hope when it is willing to fish in the daytime, in deep water. The world doesn't need another church that is content to rely on its own strength and resources. It needs believers who are unafraid to invite the power of God to work through them with demonstrations that break the boundaries and pierce the preconceptions of people who have lost all hope. As we take this risk and begin to experience His hope, we will be driven to our knees and find hope for a better life. That is the only chance for redemption for places like Germantown—and for the sin-sick community where you live.

QUESTIONS FOR DISCUSSION:

1. *Describe the spiritual needs of your own community.*
2. *How are you helping to meet these needs?*
3. *How would you evaluate how your local church is reaching your community with the love and power of Jesus?*

> *Moves of God are real; but how we apply these experiences to daily life determines their lasting value.*

MIRACULOUS LIVING

Clutching his microphone as if it were a baton, the evangelist leapt from the platform like a rock star. He proceeded to march around the sanctuary, praying more fervently with every step. As if nudged out of my seat by God's firm hand, I promptly fell in line behind him. That was my first and only "Jericho march," but it proved to be one of the most profound spiritual experiences of my life. Naturally I expected to awaken the next morning overwhelmed with excitement. Instead, I found myself battling depression. I didn't doubt the authenticity of the experience, but I became somewhat skeptical of its long-term value.

This wasn't the first time I debated the lasting impact of a spiritual experience. Years earlier, as a youth pastor, I led a retreat for the young people of our church. After the guest speaker's message on the first night, the Holy Spirit began to move among the teenagers. Kids raised their hands in worship and lifted their voices in prayer. Suddenly the room grew dark, damp and windy. I assumed a summer storm was approaching, so I slipped out the door to close the windows of our bus. To my surprise, it was perfectly calm outside.

There was no rain or hovering clouds. The storm was inside the room! I shook my head in disbelief, trying to understand what was happening. Finally I ushered my wife and several others to the door to ensure it wasn't my imagination. *This is an Upper Room experience, just like in the Book of Acts,* I told myself. *After witnessing an undeniable miracle, the people in this room will never backslide. They'll serve God the rest of their lives!*

Yet despite the emotional impact of that weekend, some of the youth fell away from God in the weeks that followed. Their tears of repentance and awe of the miraculous evaporated. They returned to their addictions to drugs, sex and alcohol. As a young minister, the episode led me to question the significance of this kind of spiritual experience. I wondered, *Why aren't moves of God sustainable? Why can't we live in the supernatural rather than having just an occasional miraculous moment?*

Years have passed since I asked those questions. And I'm still learning God's mysterious ways. But, of this

I'm certain: God is not offended by honest questions or occasional skepticism. He just doesn't want our appreciation for the miraculous to be eroded by unbelief.

Revival moments are intended to increase our faith and power in daily life. They are not intended to lead to stagnation or complacency. God doesn't want us to build shrines wherever we experience the miraculous. He doesn't want us to stay on the mountaintops after we experience emotional highs. He wants us to gain new strength to go down the mountain and minister to others. He wants our newfound faith and power to influence every aspect of our lives, wherever we go: at home, at work, at church and school. Moves of God are real, but how we apply these experiences to daily life determines their lasting value.

WHERE IS THE ADVENTURE?

Our home in Texas is located near a county park that is reserved for hiking. The first few times I took our dog, Chewbacca, on a walk there, I felt as if I were in training for an episode of *Survivor.* But when I discovered the trails merely went in a circle, I lost my sense of adventure. Now our walks are just for the exercise.

For some, Christianity has lost this sense of adventure. It began with an adrenaline rush. It may have even started with the sound of wind and flames of fire, just as the earliest Christians experienced on the Day of Pentecost. Many of us have had such experiences, but we learned to domesticate our faith into a ritual exercise. We lost the wildness of God's Spirit. We started walking in circles rather than exploring the vastness of the Holy Spirit.

God did not intend for us to walk through life on a treadmill. We have a destination! We have a God-given purpose to glorify Him and give hope to others. The writers of the New Testament call us to a different walk. We are called to "walk in love" (Ephesians 5:2, NKJV), "walk in light" (1 John 1:7, NKJV) and "walk in the Spirit" Galatians 5:25, NKJV). These phrases show us that the Christian life is truly an adventure, not a casual stroll. We should expect the miraculous. This should be "normal" for every Christian.

DON'T QUENCH THE SPIRIT

One afternoon a cracker became lodged in my throat and I started choking. I began to panic, but Beck sprang into action. Imitating a maneuver she had seen in a movie, she hit me between the shoulder blades and then employed her version of the Heimlich maneuver to remove the obstruction. I never appreciated a whack on the back like that day.

We need a similar rescue operation in the church, because many Christians—and even entire congregations—are choking out the power of the Holy Spirit. We are told in 1 Thessalonians 5:19 that we can "quench" the Holy Spirit. There are many things that can quench His power, including religious traditions, fear, pride and selfishness. We must not allow these things to choke us. When we choose to walk in wholeness, and when our body, soul and spirit are in alignment with the Holy Spirit, He can breathe life into us without interference.

Cars won't get washed and lawns won't get watered if garden hoses are kinked—regardless of the water pressure. Some Christians are like kinked garden hoses. Unless they invite God to remove the obstructions (such as unconfessed sin, bad attitudes or fears, for example) the Holy Spirit cannot flow freely.

Removing these kinks from a local church requires a diverse community as well as leaders with spiritual authority. Too often congregations are comprised of people who have the same spiritual perspectives and traditions. As a result, likeminded people choke on the same issues. Until someone with a different point of view identifies the kinks and has the courage to impose the Heimlich maneuver, the obstructions will continue. Gossip and criticism will abound, grace and mercy will be absent, and maintaining church buildings will become more important than reaching unbelievers. Spiritual kinks are the reason some churches have failed for decades to experience an authentic move of God.

Removing these obstructions begins on a personal level. Individuals must invite the Holy Spirit to remove sin, attitudes, bitterness, pride, pain and guilt. They must ask God for a fresh touch and find deliverance from the past as well as a clear vision for their future. This transformation requires faith and perseverance, because the enemy will attempt to use old patterns to limit what God wants to do in their lives and in a local congregation. Believers must cling to the hope that the Spirit will help to sustain the good work He has started.

WE NEED A BREAKTHROUGH

During our third year of marriage, Beck and I needed some major kinks removed from our relationship. We weren't communicating well with each other, nor were we allowing the Holy Spirit to bring healing into our situation. We decided that if marriage required loving your spouse, we were in serious trouble. The words we said in our wedding ceremony, "Until death do us part," simply made us feel stuck with each other.

Our internal despair finally became a cry for help. Beck asked several friends to come to our home and pray for her until she experienced a breakthrough. That day she invited the Holy Spirit to remove the debris from her life and to give her a fresh touch. Through those fervent prayers, God began a slow and steady progress. Nothing changed instantly or dramatically. Yet Beck came from her God encounter with this pronouncement: "I don't love you, but I want to want to love you."

From that day forward, you could see the conflict in action. She didn't want to kiss me or hold my hand, but she forced herself to out of her commitment to Jesus. This got my attention. Her love for Jesus morphed into a love for me, which melted my resistance. I acknowledged my own need for a personal transformation. I expressed my gratitude for what He had accomplished in Beck's heart and asked Him to do the same for me. God heard my prayer, and He replaced the disappointment of a failing marriage with hope for a godly union. Beck and I have never looked back since that day, and our love for each other has grown deeper and richer ever since.

If God can remove the kinks from a marriage, He can do the same for anyone—and for any local church. If we earnestly pray for a fresh move of God, He will respond and our lives and churches will never be the same.

QUESTIONS FOR DISCUSSION:

1. *Have you ever had an intense spiritual high that didn't last? Describe that experience.*
2. *How would you describe your walk with God? Is it a stroll—or an adventure?*
3. *We are commanded not to quench the Holy Spirit. What are some of the obstructions that tend to choke the flow of the Holy Spirit in your life?*

> *Just as one crosses the border from one country into another, we can cross into a deeper spiritual realm that allows us to hear Him with more clarity.*

HEARING GOD

As our wedding date approached, I had my share of sleepless nights and sweaty palms. I wasn't sure Beck was the one for me, and my cold feet were nearly frostbitten. While visiting my grandparents in Mississippi, I thought I heard my Grandpa call my name late one night. I crawled out of bed and put my ear to his bedroom door. But all I could hear was his rhythmic snoring.

Obviously my imagination was playing a trick on me, I told myself. I returned to bed, only to hear my name called again. *It must be my Dad,* I reasoned. I followed his snoring all the way down the hall. It was soon apparent that someone else had called my name.

As I lay awake contemplating my marriage, the absurd possibility crossed my mind it might be God who was calling for me. This was absurd because I hadn't been praying intensely, and I wasn't in a church listening to hymns in the background. I didn't feel spiritual at all. Nevertheless, I decided to play along: "God," I said, "if You have something to say to me, I'm all ears."

I wish I could say my room was instantly filled with the sound of angel voices, brilliant lights and a booming voice from heaven. Instead, a holy silence filled the room. Even the crickets stopped chirping. After convincing myself I needed a psychological assessment, I returned to combatting my wedding fears. Then a powerful thought filled my mind. I sensed the Lord saying to me, *Yes, I want you to marry Becky.*

Suddenly I knew the issue was settled. God had spoken to me. He didn't speak like I had expected, but I was absolutely certain I had heard His voice. Marrying Beck was God's will for my life.

THE CHARCOAL IS ON AISLE SIX

A few years later I found myself at another crossroads. It's probably not appropriate for ministers to say this, but I will go ahead and admit it: Sometimes the ministry sucks! I had experienced attacks on my character, a lack of appreciation for my work, huge demands on my time, unwelcome family sacrifices—all these things had piled up until the pressure became unbearable. I had endured a difficult season with little rest. Months had passed since I felt the presence of God, and faith had given way to anger. I continued to preach and perform my church duties, but all of it seemed lifeless and self-initiated. I felt completely detached from God.

One afternoon I took my bad attitude into a grocery store. Because I couldn't find the charcoal, I became irritated that the store had rearranged its floor plan without seeking my permission. I surveyed the dog food, cereal and bread aisles but refused to ask a clerk for help. My frustration grew as I wandered past new displays of insecticides, flea collars, motor oil and mayonnaise. Just when I was about to scream for help, I heard a voice over the intercom: "The charcoal is on aisle six."

At first the announcement startled me. I said to myself, *Hopefully my aggravation wasn't that obvious. But how did the announcer know I was looking for charcoal?*

Finally I concluded that Beck must have phoned the store manager, who attended our church, and asked him to make sure I purchased the right brand of charcoal. In an attempt to confirm my theory, I asked to see the manager. The assistant manager replied, "I'm sorry, John is off today." I wish I'd taken a deep breath before asking my next question: "Then who made the announcement about the charcoal in aisle six?"

She peered at me as if wondering if I had been smoking marijuana. "What announcement?" she asked. "No one made any announcement."

Honestly I didn't know God was concerned about whether I found the right brand of charcoal for our barbecue grill. Some people hear profound words from God, such as "Cross the Red Sea," "David is the next king of Israel" or "Go and preach to Caesar." But I heard God speak to me about the location of charcoal!

I struggled to explain my experience in the grocery store to others because I didn't feel I deserved God's attention at that time. I had a bad attitude. I was pouty and self-absorbed. I hadn't prayed and fasted for days leading up to the epiphany. I hadn't even asked for His help! Why should He care?

I learned in that profound moment that God sometimes communicates with us when we least expect Him to because He wants to prove He is walking with us through both good times and bad. Proverbs 15:3 (NIV) tells us: "The eyes of the Lord are everywhere." Nothing escapes His view. But He is more than a Great Spectator in the sky, watching people and their secrets. He is also the Great Communicator. He wants to converse with the people He loves. He is always speaking, but we aren't always listening.

RANDOM SENTENCES FROM GOD

A friend of mine was shopping for a new car and had taken a test drive. He admired the automobile's color, sleek design, plush interior and powerful engine. But while he turned a corner to return to the dealership, a random sentence came to his mind: *I don't want you to buy this new car.* He wrestled for a moment because this was the car of his dreams. But in the end he phoned me to say he believed God had told him to hang onto his clunker.

Fifteen minutes later, another friend called. "I've been evaluating things," she said, "and I believe God spoke to me about opening a business." I congratulated her, because who was I to question what she had heard? Later that day, a disgruntled wife informed me that God had spoken to her, too. She said God wanted her to dump her husband and marry a co-worker. This time, I seriously questioned whether God was speaking to her. I offered some counsel by saying, "That doesn't sound like God's voice to me."

I found myself intrigued and perplexed by the notion that God can speak to so many people on a wide range of topics, so I began asking Him for understanding. The Bible, I discovered, explains the process of hearing God's voice. The supernatural aspect involves fusion.

This can be seen in the life of the prophet Ezekiel, who had many dramatic encounters with the Lord. When he was first called to prophesy to Israel, he had a brilliant vision of heaven. Then God commanded Ezekiel to stand on his feet. Ezekiel wrote: "As He spoke to me the Spirit entered me and set me on my feet; and I heard Him speaking to me" (Ezekiel 2:2). This breathtaking moment was actually Ezekiel's commissioning into ministry.

The Spirit of God, described in the Bible as wind, breathes into the human spirit and the result is a new spiritual capacity. The moment of spiritual visitation—or "knowing" God's presence—accomplishes a dynamic objective: it quickens and energizes our spirit. The human spirit is temporarily connected to God's Spirit, which translates into our ability to hear His voice. Just as one crosses the border from one country into another, we can cross into a deeper spiritual realm that allows us to hear Him with greater clarity and gives more capacity for Christian living.

Without the vitality of God's Spirit influencing a

human spirit, people tend to buy cars they shouldn't, or stay in the same old job instead of venturing to start a business. They also leave their spouses instead of learning to walk in marital faithfulness. People who do unbiblical things while claiming, "God told me it was okay," are not really listening to God's voice. They are relying on their own values, emotions, ambitions, desires and fears to navigate life's decisions.

OLD VS. NEW

Fresh spiritual experiences are supposed to lead us to new spiritual practices. They impart new ideas and attitudes for daily living. But a new spiritual capacity often will create a conflict if we have become entrenched in old habits. The Hebrew word for soul can be translated neck. The human soul (our mind, will, and emotions) is a choke point for spiritual development. The breath of the Holy Spirit sometimes struggles to pass into our mind because we are unwilling to turn from our sin, repent of a bad attitude or embrace a particular spiritual discipline. The Spirit offers us a new life capacity but we must be willing to change. We cannot be "stiff-necked" or stubborn. We must exercise faith to abandon life-long patterns and affections.

Shortly after Beck and I were married, I tried to love her on my terms. When we celebrated our first Christmas I bought her a set of golf clubs even though she hates the sport. She didn't hesitate to express her disinterest in spending our evenings together on the golf course!

Soon I learned a better way to demonstrate my love: I came into her world instead of insisting she come into mine. We went shopping together, for example. At first this was agonizing because I am a "60-second shopper." I like to rush into the store, grab what I need and get home. My wife, on the other hand, enjoys strolling through the mall for hours, comparing prices and trying on clothes. My perspective changed when I saw the joy on her face as I made an effort to enter her world.

That's the way it is with God. He wants us to forsake our ways and adopt His. He wants to be intimate with us. He draws us toward what He loves because He knows those things are beneficial to our lives.

DIRECT COMMUNICATION

Some people have called the Bible a road map for life. As the revelation of God's nature and character, it certainly provides guidance for daily living. But it doesn't tell us which movie to see, which car to buy, which job to take or whom we should marry. The Bible instructs us to nurture a relationship with the Holy Spirit so that we can listen to His voice for guidance in every aspect of our lives.

The Book of Acts, in particular, emphasizes the importance of hearing from God. There are many examples of how the Lord guided the steps of people in their daily lives during the first years of the early church. In the Upper Room in Acts 2, God showed His followers that He wanted to empower them. In Acts 10, Philip was instructed by the Holy Spirit to meet with an Ethiopian eunuch and to preach to the Gentiles. In Acts 13, Paul and Barnabas were led by the Holy Spirit to take the gospel to Europe. In Acts 15, Christ's followers established church policy, saying, "It seemed good to the Holy Spirit and to us." And, in Acts

20, the Holy Spirit warned Paul about impending danger waiting for him in Jerusalem.

It was obvious that the early Christians believed the Holy Spirit was communicating directly with them. They trusted Him to guide their major decisions, including where to preach the gospel and what cities to avoid. That same Holy Spirit desires to communicate with us today. It is possible to hear His voice.

The Early Church experienced meteoric growth, in part because the Holy Spirit was in control. They took their marching orders from the One who had breathed new life into them. Had they not relied on this spiritual communication, the consequences would have been severe. Today, if we do not hear the voice of the Spirit, we simply base decisions solely upon what we see rather than on what God knows is best. We are content to live our Christian lives in a carnal way rather than in dependence on God.

Sometimes the Spirit speaks to us and we stubbornly ignore His voice because we don't like what we hear. We want to set our own course—one that suits our priorities. Obedience to the voice of the Holy Spirit often requires taking steps and making life decisions that are difficult. The Bible is full of examples of people who experienced hardship because they obeyed God's voice. They found themselves in prisons, fiery furnaces, shipwrecks, courtrooms and countless battles. But their obedience opened the doorway to God's favor and the miraculous.

When the Spirit speaks, we are invited to move beyond our insecurities and fears into a new dimension of life that is filled with hope and greater impact.

Many people ask, "How will I recognize God's voice? What does the Holy Spirit sound like?" Let me put your mind at ease: He doesn't sound like Sean Connery or James Earl Jones, although He certainly could. After all, He spoke to Balaam through a donkey (see Numbers 22:21-30). The Spirit's voice can resonate like the voice of a teacher, coach, parent or friend. Sometimes it's a voice you have never heard. But most of the time, God's utterances are not mystical, spooky or even audible. Rather they are like melodic notes being sung to your heart.

God's words are often gentle and yet always penetrating. When you really hear from Him, you almost instantly feel alive: A sentence has been highlighted in your mind and you know God has spoken. His words have the power to heal, guide and empower you. His words are both timely and precise.

Certainly some misguided Christians have taken "Spirit speak" to extremes. For these hyper-spiritual types, "hearing from God" is a phrase they leverage to get what they want. Essentially they are writing their own dialog in a one-person theatrical production while the Holy Spirit is watching from the wings. They are the stars of this show, and the Holy Spirit is not the director.

Hearing from God is not about manipulating Him to hear what you want; it's about surrendering to His perfect will. God wants us to express our love for Him, faithfully work to build His kingdom, live in obedience to His Word and love our neighbors as ourselves. As we become more intimate with Him, His voice will become more distinct. We can't force Him to speak so loudly that His voice breaks through the noise. It is our job to calm the noise of our own anxiety, fear and self-will so that we can hear Him when He does choose to speak to us.

HEALING AND FORGIVENESS

When the Holy Spirit speaks, and people listen, it opens the door to incredible possibilities. In 1994, nearly one million people were slaughtered in a matter of weeks during a tribal uprising in Rwanda. Today mass graves and mounds of human skulls are reminders of this senseless holocaust.

This horrible act of genocide was the backdrop for a conference I preached at in Africa. It was obvious that the Rwandan nightmare was still etched in their memories. One of the grieving pastors stood and asked me a question: "My family was murdered, and the men who killed them now attend my church. How can I forgive until justice is served?"

The pastors fidgeted in their chairs as I weighed my response. The atmosphere grew tense. Then the Holy Spirit gave me an answer. I said, "Until you know that Jesus' death on the cross accomplished justice for all our sins, you have no basis for forgiveness. But if you believe Christ's accomplishment was for all sin, you absorb from Christ what He made available."

Tears welled up in the eyes of the pastor and I could almost see the bitterness draining out of him. He knew the Holy Spirit had given him a word for that moment. He smiled and nodded approvingly. And I quietly thanked God for using me to speak His healing message.

During one of our church services in Texas, the Holy Spirit also spoke to a woman named Celeste about forgiving the drunk driver who had killed her sister and four of her nieces. For twenty years she was eaten up with pain and bitterness she harbored in her heart since this senseless accident. Yet after having an encounter with

God she wrote a letter of forgiveness to the man responsible for taking the lives of her loved ones. Subsequently, the letter was read at the man's parole hearing, and it resulted in the man's release.

When another woman named Miriam was told that she and her husband couldn't bear children, they continued to pray. Ultimately God favored them with twins. As Miriam shared the miracle of her pregnancy with our congregation, she also conveyed what she sensed the Holy Spirit was saying—that there would be more pregnancy miracles in our congregation. Indeed, in the next several weeks, four couples who previously were unable to conceive children learned they were pregnant!

One Sunday, a guest speaker at our church felt prompted by the Holy Spirit to tell the congregation that people with cancer would find healing at our church. Since then, we have seen people receive "category-one" healings as God supernaturally removed malignant tumors. All these miracles happened because God spoke His word!

SPIRIT-LED PEOPLE

For those just beginning to open their ears to the voice of the Spirit, I have some simple advice: Spend time with people who are Spirit-led. Don't follow people who claim to hear from God every minute or who are overtly mystical. You want to rub shoulders with people who demonstrate discipline, humility, grace and faith. If you're in the woods, for example, you should know the difference between the sound of a squirrel and the sound of a bear. Mature Christians can help you distinguish the difference between spiritual and imaginary sounds.

One of the ways to gauge the authenticity of the Spirit's voice is that He often speaks about Jesus. He reminds us of Christ's love and how the Son of God responded to situations recorded in Scripture. The Holy Spirit answers the question "What would Jesus do?" He always cuts through religious clichés and points us to the Savior. He never downplays the Son of God.

Now is the perfect time to invite the Holy Spirit to speak to you. The following prayer is a good place to begin: Holy Spirit, I welcome Your conversation with me. I'm going to listen for Your voice—when You speak to me about the issues of life or about Jesus and His love. I want to do Your will. Amen.

A multi-millionaire was asked to explain how he became so financially successful. He replied, "I just kept expanding." He always looked for new ways to learn and improve his business. As a follower of Jesus, the prayer you just offered to the Holy Spirit is an invitation for Him to expand your understanding of the Holy Spirit's voice. Learn to recognize His voice each day, and make it your goal to obey whatever He tells you.

QUESTIONS FOR DISCUSSION:

1. *Can you think of a time when you heard God clearly speak to you? Describe that experience.*

2. *Is there anything in your life that is interfering with your ability to hear God's voice?*

3. *Who in your life seems to consistently hear God's voice? What could you learn from that person?*

5

> *Nothing can transform our mood of despair into an attitude of hope like an intimate conversation with God.*

PRAYER THAT WORKS

The summer of 1977 should have been the time of my life. Instead I was miserable. I was interning as a youth worker at a church in Jacksonville, Florida, and my girlfriend, Beck, was interning in a remote fishing village in Emonak, Alaska. We were thousands of miles apart, and communication was difficult. This was years before such luxuries as cell phones, Internet and Skype. Emonak had one pay telephone in town; the church apartment where I was staying didn't even have a phone!

If someone called the church after hours, a bell would ring in my apartment. Anticipating it might be Beck, I'd unlock the doors, race through the sanctuary and try to answer before the caller hung up. Beck and I had only three conversations the entire summer.

As the days passed without a phone call, I began to wonder if Beck still loved me or if she had fallen for someone else. But all my doubts and fears subsided—and my hopes soared—every time I heard her voice.

In the same way, nothing can transform our mood of despair into an attitude of hope like an intimate conversation with God. Hope and optimism will not reside in our hearts and minds without prayer. And, sustained prayer is impossible without love. Genuine love is the syntax for prayer. The reason we choose to have conversations with Him is because we love Him and we know He loves us. Through prayer, we discover what is on God's heart, and we make His plans our priorities.

In Genesis 1, God's purpose for humankind is clearly articulated: God created man in His own image ... and God said to them, 'Be fruitful and multiply, and fill the earth, and subdue it; and rule.'" Psalm 8:3-8 reiterates this divine destiny: "When I consider Your heavens, the work of Your fingers ... What is man that You take thought of him ... Yet you have made him a little lower than God, and You crown him with glory and majesty! You make him to rule over the works of Your hands."

God created us, in part, to steward the Earth. Prayer is the method of communication whereby we receive His instructions and nurture our relationship with Him. Conversing with God is not complicated. Unlike my summer experience in Jacksonville, talking to God does not require bells, locks or sprints through the sanctuary in the early morning.

God is always listening. He is eager to respond. He never closes His ears to His children. And yet prayer is among the most underutilized tools at our disposal. Most Christians do not comprehend its power or its reach.

PRAYER THAT SHIFTS CULTURE

The Bible contains numerous accounts of how prayer changed the course of cultures. In Numbers 16, Moses discovered that his leadership was being threatened by a band of rebels led by Korah. In response, he prayed and an earthquake swallowed his detractors. Rather than respecting the fact that Moses had a direct line to God Almighty, the rebellious Children of Israel rose up against him for killing Korah. The rebellion released a death plague into the camp, which put the entire nation at risk.

In the midst of this calamity, Moses prayed for God's forgiveness and mercy:

"Moses said to Aaron, Take Your censer and put in it fire from the altar, and lay incense on it, then bring it quickly to the congregation and make atonement for them ... The plague has begun! Then Aaron took it as Moses had spoken, and ran into the midst of the assembly ... and made atonement for the people. He took his stand between the dead and the living, so that the plague was checked" (Numbers 16:46-48).

The use of the censer and incense was symbolic of Moses' prayer and worship. His prayers brought life where there was death, and hope in place of despair. If Moses' prayers could bring healing to an entire nation under the limitations of the Old Covenant (before the coming of Jesus Christ), surely our persistent prayers today can restore health to those who are suffering with AIDS, cancer and other diseases. Under the New Covenant, the power of prayer is limitless!

In his letter to the Galatians, the apostle Paul wrote of his disappointment that believers had strayed from Christ's teachings. He scolded them by saying, "O foolish Galatians! Who has bewitched you that you should not obey the truth?" (Galatians 3:1, NKJV).

Fortunately, Paul did not give up on the Galatian disciples. In Galatians 4:19 (NKJV), he wrote, "My little children, for whom I labor in birth again until Christ is formed in you." Paul believed he could play a role in restoring the church by "laboring," which is another term for intense praying. Like a woman who endures the pain of childbirth, Paul positioned himself to "labor," or pray, for the church to return to the ways of Christ.

If Paul's agonizing travail could change the course of an entire congregation, our prayers can help change the direction of classmates, fellow employees, neighbors and family members. We must not give up on them. We must continue believing in prayer.

In 1 Kings 18:20-40, Elijah, the prophet of God, watched painfully as his culture traded hope in God for faith in the mythological god Baal. In the midst of a prolonged drought, the people turned to Baal because they believed this mythological being controlled the forces of nature. Elijah called for a showdown: Baal versus God.

The prophets of Baal raised their voices and fell prostrate before their idol. Elijah simply prayed for the

God of heaven to demonstrate His power. In the end, the true God stole the show. Baal didn't even make an appearance, even though his followers desperately cut themselves to manipulate him into sending rain.

But the story didn't end with that victory. The nation still needed rain, so Elijah climbed a mountain to pray. As Elijah persevered in prayer, he asked his servant to peer into the sky for rain clouds. "See anything yet?" Elijah asked. "Nothing," the servant replied.

Elijah continued to pray, crouching with his head between his knees. The Bible says he was in a birthing position! As he groaned in prayer he repeatedly sent his servant on scouting expeditions to look for any sign of a downpour. Finally, on the seventh trip, the servant spotted a small, dark cloud in the distance. That cloud was the answer to Elijah's prayers. If one man's prayers can bring needed rain to a backslidden nation, our prayers can bring multiplied breakthroughs to our finances, relationships, emotions and health.

MUSTARD SEEDS OF FAITH

Matthew 17 tells the story of a demon-possessed boy who threw himself into fire and water because of seizures. Neither medical doctors nor Christ's disciples could offer a solution. But when Jesus rebuked the demon, the boy was completely delivered. Subsequently Jesus showed the secret of helping people find hope, saying, "If you have faith as a mustard seed, you will say to this mountain, 'Move from here to there,' and it will move; and nothing will be impossible for you" (Matthew 17:20, NKJV).

I never really cared for this verse, to be honest. When I read it I felt condemned. I desperately wanted to believe what it says, but quite frankly I hadn't heard of any mountains that were relocated in the last 2,000 years. (I tried moving a mountain with my mind when I was a kid and nothing happened.) I suppose we can classify Jesus' words as a metaphor, but He made it sound so simple. Could you imagine the impact if just one Christian stood at the base of one mountain and it moved—even just a little?

Yet I gained deeper insight into this analogy during a trip to Palm Springs, California, where Beck and I rode the world's steepest gondola. In a matter of minutes we soared from the hot desert to a frigid mountaintop. We shivered all the way up because we were wearing only shorts and T-shirts. All the way up the mountain I noticed that it was made of impenetrable granite, except for some peculiar pockets of trees. I asked myself, *How do trees grow in such rocky terrain?*

Like a word from heaven, this answer came to me: The mountain moved. Somehow, a seed found its way into a crevasse as wind or a bird carried it. And, over time, the pressure of life inside the seed germinated and produced forests rising from granite!

Jesus said it and I believe it: We can move mountains. Prayer works! The plans and purposes of the Holy Spirit abide inside of us, and they are just waiting to be planted—even in the hardest hearts and deadest churches. Death plagues aren't just ancient fables. Neither are bewitched churches or extended droughts. Our children are as much at risk as the boy Jesus delivered from seizures and demonic influence. So what should we do? Do we simply wring our hands and say, "What will be will be?" No, that only leads to more despair. Breakthroughs come through the persistent prayers of faith. Breakthroughs come because we believe prayer works.

QUESTIONS FOR DISCUSSION:

1. *Describe your present prayer life, and how you would like to see it change.*
2. *What is the biggest need in your life right now? Do you honestly believe prayer could change your circumstances?*
3. *What steps can you take to devote more time to prayer and less energy to worry?*

> *As children of God, we are not victims of our circumstances. And we do not live at the mercy of this world.*

GRINNING IN CHAINS

One morning I was praying with intensity about a problem I was facing, when I heard myself say, "God I'll do anything to experience more of You."

At that moment, it seemed like God offered a humorous response. I heard Him say: *Then roll across the room.*

Of course, I told myself, *God would never ask me to do something as silly as that.* So I simply continued praying: "God, I'll do anything to live in Your strong anointing."

Again I sensed God responding: *Then roll across the room.* I replied, "God, if that's You speaking to me, I can't believe You're asking me to roll my way into Your favor." It took about five full 360-degree rolls to get to the other side of the room. I know this seems far-fetched, but when I did this simple act of obedience I experienced God's presence in a powerful way.

Every time I tell this story, I worry that people will take it to extremes and try to roll their way into intimacy with God. For me, this was a one-time experience and not a pattern for others to follow. I'm not completely sure why God asked me to roll, but the episode sparked spiritual momentum that has continued for years.

Here's one explanation: I believe God wanted me to experience Him on His terms—not mine. Prior to that morning, I thought I was spiritually loaded and fully abandoned to God. Yet this odd experience helped me laugh at my illusions of self-importance and, strangely, it taught me to have more fun with God!

Did you know God is playful? Zephaniah 3:17 says He will "exult over you with joy" and that He rejoices over us "with shouts of joy." The New International Version translates it this way: "He will ... rejoice over you with singing."

God takes pleasure in our laughter and promises to help us smile even when we feel chained to a bad job, a low-performing marriage or a debilitating disease. We can grin in the midst of our circumstances knowing that our difficult trials are no match for God's power. Hope always comes to us on His terms, not ours!

CITIZENS' RIGHTS

Paul was certainly no stranger to difficult circumstances. He lived many months of his life in dark, rat-infested prison cells. He knew the bruising and discoloration caused by shackles on his wrists and ankles. In Acts 22:24-29, a Roman guard interrogated Paul and was about to commence torture when the apostle abruptly called a time-out. He basically asked, "Does it matter that I'm a Roman citizen?"

The guard was horrified. The game changed the moment he realized his prisoner had the rights of a Roman citizen. Suddenly the commander of Rome's army was apologizing to an inmate! Perhaps he offered some food to Paul and tried to change the subject to discussions about politics or the latest gladiator contest. In light of Paul's Roman citizenship, he was no longer a prisoner—he was a Roman comrade. How did this happen? Paul simply invoked the authority of a greater city against the authority of a lesser city. Rome and Jerusalem clashed in Paul's cell and Rome came out the winner.

What does this mean for us? We are citizens of the kingdom of God. The ultimate authority is not limited to some city on earth. God's kingdom has jurisdiction over every other nation. For that reason, Jesus taught us to invoke our rights as citizens of God's kingdom, to appeal to a higher authority regardless of our circumstances. He said to pray this way: "Your kingdom come Your will be done, on earth as it is in heaven" (Matthew 6:10). Jesus told us to invoke our rights as God's rightful heirs!

As children of God, we are not victims of our circumstances. And we do not live at the mercy of this world. Instead we can live with the hope of eternity and carry out our daily duties while Almighty God, the greatest authority in the universe, guards our backs. We belong to His kingdom and He promises to protect and preserve us as His ambassadors.

There are three ways to visit a country: as a tourist, an immigrant or an ambassador. Tourists often pay too much for food and lodging, and immigrants are often required to transfer their citizenship (and if they sneak in without proper documentation they can be deported). Ambassadors, on the other hand, enjoy the full rights, protections and privileges of a country without becoming subservient. Paul saw believers as "Christ's ambassadors" to the world. (See 2 Corinthians 5:20.) The hope that allows us to grin in chains comes from an understanding of our ambassadorship (or transcendent existence) and intimacy with the Creator of the universe.

A BUZZ LIGHTYEAR ATTITUDE

Do you remember Buzz Lightyear, the likeable plastic space ranger from *Toy Story*? He had such a positive outlook on life. Regardless of his predicament, even when he and his friends from the toy box were in peril, his anthem was always, "To infinity and beyond!"

Some people are just like Buzz. They seem to soar despite inclement weather, illness or unpaid bills. They appear to have an edge, as if they have a supply of secret resources to help them conquer the villains of life. Their hope springs eternal even when circumstances are dark. Conversely, others seem to pass through life as victims of the lies and schemes of the devil. They haven't taken advantage of the enormous privileges that come along with the gift of salvation.

As a six-year-old boy growing up in Montgomery, Alabama, I had earned a reputation as the worst baseball player at Flowers Elementary. Whenever I approached the plate, I led the Flowers Blue team in strikeouts. I just couldn't understand why God gave some kids the ability to hit and throw and not me.

When our family relocated to Columbus, Georgia, my father took me to meet my new Little League coach. The coach asked my dad if I was a good baseball player. "He's great!" my father said. At that moment I knew my dad was either a convincing liar or a man of great faith. "Terrific—what position does he play?" the coach asked. Dad replied, "What position do you need?"

Now, we're both in loads of trouble, I said to myself. The coach scratched his head, saying, "I could sure use a starting pitcher for today's game." Dad didn't hesitate to offer my services, even though my pitching experience was limited to playing catch with him in the backyard. "You're in luck—Jimmy is a great pitcher," he said.

When I marched to the mound in our first practice, panic set in. *We're both going to be called liars,* I told myself. I'm not sure if it was Dad's faith or my prayers that converged on that mound, but something supernatural happened. I threw a perfect game. And from that day forward, I became an above average baseball player.

My dad believed in me, and his faith and encouragement changed my game. In the same way, God believes in you more than you believe in yourself! Throughout the course of your life, your Father is announcing your transcendent potential just like He did for Moses, David, Mary and Paul. They led nations to freedom, defeated giants, gave birth to the Savior of the world, and planted churches throughout the Roman Empire simply because they submitted their futures to the God of the universe.

Sometimes people who feel disqualified or under-prepared are, in God's eyes, the most qualified. They may feel terribly insecure, but their weakness forces them to look to God for strength. They discover the secret of transcendence. They are able to say with the apostle Paul: "It is no longer I who live, but Christ lives in me" (see Galatians 2:20).

This transcendence has little to do with us, and more to do with God and His unlimited power and resources. Transcendence looks at life and says, *I know I'm in chains,* or, *I know I've got a poor performance record,* or, *I know what the doctor diagnosed.* This person will simply not allow hardship or failure to define their lives. Instead, they say: *I live as a citizen of a greater city, with power from another world.* We can endure chains if we have the right perspective. Instead of interpreting God based on our circumstances, we must interpret our circumstances according to who God is and how much He loves us.

WE NEED A SECOND TOUCH

After healing the blind man at Bethsaida, Jesus asked him to describe what he saw. He told Jesus, "I see men like trees' walking" (see Mark 8:22-26, NKJV). Jesus prayed again, and the man's sight was completely restored. Have you ever wondered why this miracle required two prayers? To answer that question we must examine the context and the message Jesus was sending to His disciples.

Jesus had recruited His disciples and was training them in the ways of God. They had witnessed a few miracles and listened to Christ's teachings, but it was quickly apparent they had a long way to go to comprehend the power and authority connected to Christ's Sonship. Some were satisfied with simply hanging around Jesus. They were enticed by their new job title, the adulation of the crowds, the inspirational stories and the possibility that they might sit beside Jesus in heaven. But Jesus knew their faith was weak, and they still had much to learn.

When Jesus asked the disciples to feed the crowd of five thousand, for example, they rolled their eyes in disbelief. Moments later, Jesus multiplied the fish and bread and the hungry multitude had a feast. And yet the disciples still didn't fully understand the miracle that had occurred right before their eyes. Mark 6:52 (NKJV) says they were "amazed in themselves beyond measure, and marveled. For they had not understood about the loaves, because their heart was hardened."

Jesus was annoyed by their lack of faith and sent them out on a boat while He remained behind to pray. Later, as a storm approached and fear invaded the disciples' hearts, Jesus came to them—walking on the water! If I had seen Jesus walking on water, I'd assume He could multiply bread and fish, too. But two chapters later, in Mark 8, Jesus asked the disciples to feed another crowd of four thousand who had gathered to hear Him teach. In response, the disciples asked, "'But where in this remote place can anyone get enough bread to feed them?' Jesus asked them. 'Why are you talking about having no bread? Do you still not understand? Are your hearts hardened? Do you have eyes but fail to see, and ears but fail to hear? And don't you remember?'" (Mark 8:4,17,18, NIV).

Shortly after chastising His faithless followers, Jesus healed the blind man with the double touch. Jesus used this encounter to send a message to His disciples. He was explaining that they were stuck between touches. They had become satisfied with only a single touch of His power. But there was a second touch for them to seek and to experience.

Today many of us have become satisfied with the first touch, when God longs to touch us again! Like the blind man, we want to see clearly. But this will require a second touch from Jesus. To receive that touch, God may require some of us to roll across the room. For others, He may urge them to lift their voices in praise at a time when the chains of life are threatening to steal their joy. For still others, it may require another trip to the altar, a phone call to a friend or a simple decision to resist temptation.

Whatever the case, God has more for you than you ever imagined. Don't settle for anything less than His best for you.

QUESTIONS FOR DISCUSSION:

1. *How do you typically respond when circumstances don't go your way? Do you play the victim, or do you demonstrate faith and courage?*

2. *Paul was released from chains when he reminded the jailer that he was a Roman citizen. What are your rights as a believer in Christ?*

3. *The blind man had to receive prayer from Jesus twice to be healed. In what areas of your life do you need a second touch?*

> *"Our reality is not determined by the way things appeur, bul by what we imagine can happen when God intervenes."*

LASTING HOPE

Sightseeing on an African animal preserve was like taking a guided tour of heaven. The driver of our Jeep led us across the exotic greenbelts so Beck and I, and the other tourists, could see hippos wading in rivers, zebras retreating across plains and birds circling in multi-colored skies. Our guide asked us, "Are there any animals in particular you'd like to see?" One passenger didn't hesitate, saying, "Yeah—a leopard."

Our driver politely informed us that leopards are rarely seen in the park. The other passengers subsequently added their requests to the list: lions, buffalo, rhinos, giraffes, elephants with babies, and more.

Later that day, to everyone's astonishment, we saw a large leopard walking toward our Jeep. In fact, the large cat circled our Jeep like a model posing for photographs. If that wasn't enough, we saw every other animal on our wish list, too. Even the guide was amazed. He said that in thirty years as a sightseeing guide he had never witnessed a week like ours. He said it was almost miraculous.

Beck and I smiled at each other and nodded. We had a sense that God was shepherding the animals in our direction. From that point we dubbed our experience "leopard faith." I wish I could capture the formula for leopard faith and export it to America, but thus far that hasn't happened. But I keep looking.

We wouldn't have had that experience if we hadn't gone to an African animal preserve. It's unlikely that I'll drive up to a crosswalk in my neighborhood in Cedar Hill and spot a rhino! Likewise, hope is stirred when we deliberately place ourselves in the neighborhood where hope resides and we actively search for it. People won't find lasting hope in bars, theaters, boardrooms or cultic temples. They'll find it wherever Christ's followers are gathered.

This is one of life's undeniable lessons: You see what you look for, and you look for what you love. Beck and I can travel the same highway and she'll spot every outlet mall. Meanwhile, I'll see every boat dealership. We see and hope for what we love. But occasionally, as Christians, we love and hope for the wrong things. We must understand that hope is the natural by-product of intimacy with God. It's the inevitable confidence that comes from knowing He's literally with us. Thus, we're only hopeless if we make decisions that separate us from the love of God.

Believers often tell one another to "trust God," "praise God" and "obey God." The advice is perfectly sound, but it's also incomplete. Trust, praise and obedience are not the goal; they are natural outcomes from our love for God. And loving God is the by-product of knowing God. Seeking God leads to knowing Him, which produces love. An awareness of God also brings hope. So, our primary responsibility for spiritual development and growth is to seek Him with all our hearts. (See 1 Chronicles 22:9; Jeremiah 29:13; Deuteronomy 4:28-30.)

When I fish in Florida I always hire a professional guide. I've fished with my friend Van for 22 years because he's been trained to see fish. He considers the water temperature, measures the wind and even notices the ripples in the water. It's almost as if he sees beneath the surface. In a similar way, as our intimacy with God grows, we gain easier access to the Holy Spirit, who sees beneath the surface of life. As a result, we live full of hope, knowing the Holy Spirit will guide us through every difficulty.

Life doesn't happen without moments of desperation: betrayals, financial setbacks, illnesses and loss. The apostle Paul certainly had his tough moments, too. But, in 2 Corinthians 7, he says he has a different perspective. In verse 5 he says he was "afflicted on every side," but in verse 16 (NKJV) he says, " I rejoice ... in everything."

Paul's buoyancy of hope can be ours, but it requires frequent reminders that our problems and predicaments will turn out all right. These may come in the form of sermons, songs or encouraging words from friends. Hope requires confidence that our current sufferings merely leverage the future, that distress drives us to intimacy with God, and that pain jolts us from destructive habits to more productive, God-honoring behavior.

A NEW WAY

In Matthew 22:23-33, the Sadduccees saw an opportunity to silence Jesus because His popularity threatened their power base. They endeavored to entrap Him with a question about marriage and divorce. They assumed that Christ's answer would incite one group or another to rise up against Him.

Yet Jesus discerned their manipulative intentions and challenged the value of their debate. They were searching for loopholes in the Law when they should have been seeking a Savior to free them from their sinfulness. The self-righteous Sadduccees failed to understand that Jesus didn't come to Earth primarily to offer moral teaching or philosophical lectures or to form a political movement. He radically invaded Earth with redemptive power to establish a new way of life—a kingdom not of this world. He demonstrated love and power, cast out demons, healed the sick, brought dignity to the disenfranchised, liberated captives, destroyed evil, raised the dead and provided a true basis for hope. The greatest power in the universe is not destructive; it is redemptive. The greatest strength is not death; it is life.

Christ's strategy for bringing hope to a broken world was to recruit influencers. He told them: "Follow Me, and I will make you fishers of men" (Matthew 4:19). The way we live our lives reveals whom we are following.

Our attitudes and actions trace back to our Leader and our Teacher.

But following Jesus offers one inevitable challenge: He will confront the way we live. Some people say, "I'll follow Jesus as long as He lets me have what I want." But this type of faith is fundamentally flawed because it leaves us at the helm of our lives. And no one is intelligent or talented enough to navigate the challenges of this broken world alone. Until we decide to be a true disciple of Jesus, true hope will evade us.

Jesus diagnosed our main hindrance to hope as "hard-heartedness." This is a condition in which we assume we are under-resourced and under-qualified to address the challenges of life. Hard-hearted people don't expect God to help them.

The greatest followers of Jesus made the least assumptions. Joshua didn't assume the sun couldn't stand still. Peter didn't assume he couldn't walk on water. Mary didn't assume the wedding had to proceed without wine. Paul didn't assume that a snake's bite would automatically kill him. In each of these situations, God performed miracles because ordinary people stretched their faith and believed for the impossible. Our reality is not determined by the way things appear, but by what we imagine can happen when God intervenes.

How we view the future determines the way we live today. Imagine two farmers who own similar tracts of land, plant the same seed and use similar cultivating techniques. One of the farmers hopes to be a millionaire. The other believes bankruptcy is inevitable. Which farmer is more likely to have a better attitude? Which one will enjoy toiling the ground? Of course, the farmer who anticipates a great reward will be more likely to achieve it.

Hope anticipates God's reward.

The only way we lose is if we quit. If we find ourselves overwhelmed with uncontrollable circumstances, that's when we have to let hope spring up in our hearts. We must keep believing.

Jesus didn't come to Earth to enter your story or mine. Rather, He came so we could enter His. When we enter His story, the world doesn't suddenly turn golden, and all problems don't disappear. But every circumstance becomes an opportunity to be interpreted in light of His flourishing glory.

In the midst of today's economic turmoil, political upheaval, moral scandal, scientific absurdity, educational mutiny and the breakdown of the family, God wants hope to arise in our hearts. Allow the Holy Spirit to fill you with hope!

QUESTIONS FOR DISCUSSION:

1. *How does your view of the future impact how you live today?*

2. *Describe a difficult time in your life when God helped you overcome.*

3. *Jesus said those who lacked faith had hard hearts. In what areas do you struggle to believe God?*

Who do you have surrounding you that will give you godly counsel and words of hope when the enemy is threatening from every side?

BELONGING

Even though I do not endorse the values portrayed in the television show *M.A.S.H.*, I have to admit the final episode brought a tear to my eye. Over the years, all the program's characters—Hawkeye, B.J., Father Mulcahy, Hot Lips, Colonel Potter and Radar—had become like family to me. At times I had to remind myself they were actors filming a television show in Palm Springs.

But the long-running series smartly portrayed the affection the characters had for one another while enduring years of heartache and conflict. When they bid farewell to one another in the final episode, their emotions were torn: They longed to return to America but suddenly realized they would miss the bonds of friendship they had found in war-torn Korea.

Conflict, challenges and shared experiences have a way of forging meaningful relationships. When you link arms with someone in battle, your reliance on that person grows, as well as your need for them. This is why the bond between war veterans is so strong. We all need friends with us when we are in the trenches.

Ask yourself: Whom are you taking into battle that will guard your back and shoulder some of the load? Whom do you have surrounding you that will give you godly counsel and words of hope when the enemy is threatening from every side? The people you have alongside you will influence the outcome of the battles you face.

A few years ago Beck and I heard about a tremendous outpouring of God's Spirit in another city, so we accompanied friends to the meeting. Immediately we felt the presence of God in the church. That's why I was astonished when a friend leaned over in the middle of the service and said, "I hope we never have a church like this."

At first I didn't understand. People were being touched, backsliders were repenting and people seemed to be experiencing life-changing miracles. But my friend noticed something I had missed: There was a lack of friendship in the auditorium. A crowd had gathered, but virtually everyone was a guest. There was no lasting connection between the participants.

This revival was an amazing event, but I realized it could not replace the local church's role in building a close-knit army that could go to war against the enemy of this world. One of the benefits of belonging to a church is that it provides an extended family that will provide added protection against the evil one. Jesus did not tell us to assemble crowds, nor did He tell us that crowds could defeat the devil. Instead, He told us in Matthew 16:18 that the gates of hell would not prevail against the Church!

WELCOME TO THE WILDERNESS

The Book of Hebrews chronicles how a group of Jews had embraced Jesus as the Messiah. But when the enemy entered into battle for their souls, and trials came their way, they wanted to revert to Judaism, a much more comfortable and longstanding identity for them. Their confidence in Christianity wavered because they expected easier and more palpable change. With Jesus, they assumed life would be easier.

The author of Hebrews recognizes that their faith is fading, so he writes a letter urging them to hold on tightly to their faith, look to Jesus and remember His promises. The author recounts how the Children of Israel—the ancestors of the early Christians—had grown weary in the wilderness and quit on God. Consequently they forfeited His blessing.

Wilderness happens after you cross the Red Sea, sing a few worship choruses about an awesome God and then discover that life on the other side isn't what you imagined. It's the conflict between the way you think things should be and the way things really are. Today we live in a wilderness of disappointment—a world incompatible with our deepest longings for bodies that never get sick, beauty that lasts forever, peace that prevails, and unfailing love. Instead of these ideals we find sickness, conflict and difficulty.

Despair in the wilderness is the emotion that people like Daniel, Esther and Jeremiah experienced when their instincts told them they should be home in Jerusalem instead of living under the oppressive regime of some hostile, tax-too-much, government. Wilderness is marriage without romance, or work without the blessings of prosperity. Wilderness is when your dreams for your children disintegrate because they've made poor decisions. Wilderness is facing the trials of life without supportive friends by your side.

Wilderness was the primary context for spiritual growth for many leaders in the Bible. Consider Abraham, Isaac, Jacob, Joseph, Moses, Joshua, Deborah, Gideon and David. So many characters in the Bible went to school in this desolate place. Even Jesus was led into the wilderness! It is a training ground. The wilderness was where all these Bible characters made their most crucial decisions. In the wilderness they grew closer to God and to one another. For them the wilderness was not a curse; it was a place of holy preparation.

The dangers of a wilderness experience are dying, denying, quitting, despising and departing—what Hebrews 3:10 refers to as letting your heart go astray. It was in the wilderness that the Children of Israel stopped worshipping God and tried to displace Him with a golden calf. They took their futures into their own hands. But in the end, it was in the wilderness that they encountered God and became a nation.

Our wilderness is filled with adversity as well as opportunity. So how can we survive in it? How can we receive God's promises while we endure the harshness of this place? How can our fledgling faith be preserved in hostile territory? In a sense, the writers of *M.A.S.H.* and the author of Hebrews deliver the same prescription: If you find yourself in a war in the wilderness, you need friends you can trust.

NO MORE LONE RANGERS

The Bible emphasizes, from cover to cover, the critical role friends play in our spiritual development. That's why isolating ourselves from other believers and nurturing a relationship with Jesus alone is not a proper course. We are commanded to make relationships a priority. God never called us to be Lone Rangers. The author of Hebrews said, "Exhort one another daily" ... "so that none of you will be deceived by sin and hardened against God" (Hebrews 3:13, NKJV/NLT).

Wilderness experiences require the combination of two spiritual forces to get us through difficult times. The first is Jesus, by His Spirit, breathing into our spirits new capacity. The second involves friends who exhort, encourage, correct and nudge.

I once agreed to listen to a salesman pitch a timeshare condominium simply because he promised to reward me with a brand-new set of the latest Taylormade golf clubs. What a deal! All I had to do was listen to his hour-long speech and I could have the clubs. I was about to turn down his too-good-to-be-true offer when a manager appeared from behind an office curtain.

The chemistry between us was truly remarkable. We found acres of common ground. We knew the same people and were raised in the same part of the country. He even handed me a jar of his grandma's pickle relish! I knew he didn't expect me to purchase the timeshare, but out of a sense of friendship and loyalty I purchased it anyway. And I never heard from him again. I guess this was a reminder that some people want to be your friend only to the degree they find you useful.

Those are not the types of friends we need in church. Meaningful friendships are rare in our culture, especially the kind we need when we are in the wilderness. We need romantic love to propagate the race and we need neighborly love because society only exists if we share resources and civic responsibility. But the value of genuine friendship has been minimized in our culture. Other relationships, like timeshare companies, push themselves onto us with manipulation and hype; but true friendships can't be forced or faked; they have to be mined. We must intentionally seek out relationships that will build us up when the enemy is working to tear us down.

On the night before Jesus died, He tried to communicate the meaning of the Cross to His disciples. He said, "No longer do I call you slaves, for the slave does not know what his master is doing; but I have called you friends, for all things that I have heard from My Father I have made known to you. Greater love has no one than this, that one lay down his life for his friends" (John 15:15,13). We should be awestruck that the King of Glory calls us friends; and we should be inspired by His command to lay down our lives for our friends.

Perhaps Christian friendships are suffering today because we have become enamored with privacy. Most people live in isolation and have lost all sense of community. Friends contemplate divorce while we remain silent. Others battle depression and we let them wallow in hopelessness. Friends' reputations are attacked and we fail to come to their defense. With friends like that, who needs enemies? At best, our friendships are lazy. At worst, we've become independent and self-centered in the way we practice our faith.

FRIENDS ON THE SAME JOURNEY

Myrl Allinder is one of the most unique men I've ever met. He retired a decorated Marine colonel, having flown harrowing combat missions during the Vietnam War. We didn't have a lot in common, so I asked him why we were friends. He replied, "Because we're going to the same place." He wasn't necessarily referring to heaven. Rather, he was talking about our mutual quest to see the church move beyond institutional religion to being a family of believers that walks with God's power and presence.

Remember Sam and Frodo, the two main characters in J.R.R. Tolkien's epic tale *Lord of the Rings*? When the two hobbits agreed to take on the mission to save the world by delivering the mysterious One Ring to Mordor, they knew they had signed up for battle, danger and adventure as well as some laughter. But little did they know it was their inseparable loyalty that would ultimately save everyone in Middle Earth.

Christians are notorious for clustering around people who think and talk like them, sing the same songs, and vote for the same candidates. It makes for harmony but it runs the risk of becoming an exclusive club. (Not to mention the fact that such uniformity is boring!) It's like the tree house we built just for our buddies when we were kids. Organized religion often pulls up the ladder and says, *No one allowed except people like us.*

Yet when people accept the mission of God's kingdom, and they take the risk of opening their lives to each other regardless of racial, cultural and personality differences, true friendships are allowed to form and flourish. We are a motley crew: Some of us are rough, tempestuous and extroverted; others are shy and conservative; we are old and young, black and white, Democrat and Republican, urban and rural. How can such a diverse group rescue the world? It's simple. When we truly love each other, as Jesus taught us, we establish friendships around our common mission and exhort one another into the promised places.

Remember *The Andy Griffith Show*? Why didn't Sheriff Andy Taylor fire his klutzy deputy, Barney Fife? After all, Barney lost the keys to the jail, arrested innocent citizens and allowed crooks to escape. Andy kept Barney around, despite his mistakes, because they were such close friends. As a result, Barney fumbled his way into arrests of notorious criminals and contributed to the idyllic life of Mayberry, North Carolina.

In the same way, Jesus tolerates our failures because we are His friends. He is not in the business of firing friends. In fact, He'd prefer to deputize millions more to spread His message of love, hope and friendship. But Jesus does not seek intimacy with us just so we can be useful to Him. He wants a deep relationship so He can be more useful to us! Greater intimacy results in more guidance, power and love. Friendship is important to Jesus because He wants the people He died for to know the depth of His love.

We accept His invitation for friendship because we are grateful for His work on the cross. We've read the stories of His life, and we know He can perform the miraculous. We've watched Him work in the lives of people today. So, like the fishermen, tax collectors, prostitutes and even some religious zealots who followed Jesus, we are compelled to follow Him as well. We too want to go where He goes—even if we must pass through a wilderness to get there.

WE'VE LOST OUR 'STICKINESS'

Friendship comes before marriage. Unfortunately, in some marriages, friendship gets buried under unrealistic expectations, disappointment, selfishness, betrayal and pain. The couple loses a key ingredient that is necessary in any meaningful friendship: stickiness. Proverbs 18:24 says: "A friend ... sticks closer than a brother." At one time or another, a successful marriage or friendship requires that we "stick it out" with someone.

Remember the last wedding ceremony you attended? Chances are, during the ceremony the bride and groom were not thinking about the words they were saying or the covenants of friendship they were making. They were wishing they could jump right into the honeymoon. At one wedding I attended, the groom was so nervous he threw up three times, once on the bride!

Fortunately, traditional marriage vows have nothing to do with how nervous or queasy the bride and groom feel during the ceremony. Vows focus on future behavior—how the couple will serve one another in "sickness and health, for richer or poorer." That's their promise to walk through the wilderness—and to save the world together. "My Prince Charming!" and "My Cinderella!" won't work when we go through the tough times; that is when we must call each other "friends in mission."

Jesus is calling His bride, the Church, to this same level of "sticky" commitment. He commands us to love each other as true friends through disappointments, disagreements, failure and misunderstandings so that our common mission can be fulfilled.

Of course, when we feel the sting of betrayal and suffer attacks on our reputation, it is easy to set aside the vows of friendship. How quickly we can change a perpetrator's designation from "friend" to "enemy." That's why, in Matthew 5:44, Jesus said, "Love your enemies." He knows the enemy's plan of attack: to weaken our resolve and thwart our mission by destroying friendships and dividing churches. But Jesus also knows the enemy is no match for friendships founded in Christ.

SHEPHERDS ARE NEEDED

The Bible describes humans as sheep. Many people naturally assume sheep are like the clean and cuddly stuffed animals all children love. In fact, sheep are unintelligent, obstinate, dirty, and infested with lice and ticks! Sheep also bite! When most animals get lost they usually find their way home. Not sheep. They'll stay lost until someone comes to their rescue. Sheep are needy animals.

Like sheep, you and I need a Divine Shepherd who constantly watches over His flock. But we also need our fellow sheep to make sure we don't get lost in the first place. Jesus saves, but so do His friends. Think about it: How many times has a friend saved you from a mistake, come to your rescue or challenged your bad attitude with loving correction? How many times has a word of counsel or a timely gift helped you overcome a difficult challenge?

In parts of Alaska, some trees thrive in the tundra even though the ground is frozen a few feet below the surface. The winds in the region sometimes blow ninety miles per hour, yet these trees withstand the force. How do they do it? They entangle! They wrap their roots around the roots of other trees and hold on.

We all need the same type of support system. Whom have you authorized to rescue you when you are about to make a serious mistake? Sooner or later, something will try to uproot us with more power than we have strength to resist, and unless we "entangle" with our friends the windstorm could knock us down. We all need someone who will take ownership of our lives and say, "I'm not listening to you now. I'm going to make sure you do the right thing. I embrace the true you, not the temporarily insane person who is falling to these winds of temptation." True friends know when to entangle.

Here are four principles of friendship to help you weather the storms of life:

1. Avoid intimate relationships with people who use you or try to send you in the wrong direction. Don't be afraid to "unfriend."

2. Live realistically and boldly, even though you have doubts about your ability to nurture friendship. Because you have the ultimate Friend, Jesus Christ, you can confidently extend the hand of friendship to others.

3. Cultivate friendship with Jesus. Walk alongside Him as together you seek to fulfill His mission.

4. Stay in step with the Holy Spirit. Listen to His voice. Speak truth and offer help to those He leads into your life.

QUESTIONS FOR DISCUSSION:

1. *Who do you have surrounding you to hold you accountable and to help you make good decisions?*
2. *Describe a time when you felt you were walking in a wilderness. How were you tempted to give up during that time?*
3. *Why do you think most people, even many Christians, don't have deep, authentic friendships?*

9

> *Because of God's nature and unyielding love for us, He remains faithful even when we are not faithful to Him.*

RENEWED PURPOSE

Trinity Church was riding a wave of "success" in Cedar Hill. It had earned a place of influence in the community and was widely known for its massive Easter productions. Parking lots were full on Sundays and the church's finances were strong. Everyone could feel the momentum building. Then, tragically, one of the pastors was discovered in a secret immoral relationship that became front-page news. The church was devastated and church members left in droves. As a result, offerings dried up.

This was the church I inherited when I accepted the pastorate in 1994. I wish I could say the church bounced back quickly under my leadership, but it took seven years before the pain from the ordeal began to subside and we were able to refocus on the church's future. Finally, the congregation emerged with a fresh vision and renewed vitality.

After years of living on the brink of disaster, I was elated to be the pastor of a healthy church. So, it was surprising when I found myself sliding into a deep spiritual funk—an emotional quagmire characterized by dullness of heart, irritation and impatience. I was ready to snap.

While in this rut I attended a leadership conference and, subconsciously, began comparing myself to large ministries in Dallas: churches led by men such as T.D. Jakes, Ed Young, Tony Evans, Jack Graham, Steve Hill and others. "God," I whined, "send me someplace that's less competitive; let me go where mediocrity is appreciated."

In retrospect, I'm sure my pitiful prayers irritated God that night. Yet He patiently reminded me I had been chosen for a purpose and that He had more to accomplish if I would allow Him to correct my attitude. He did not call me to be T.D. Jakes, Steve Hill or Tony Evans. He called me to be me, and to lead Cedar Hill under His divine direction. He spoke to me clearly during the service, downloading four core values for my life and the ministry of Trinity Church.

These values are: 1) Substance, 2) Covenant Relationships, 3) Legacy and 4) Marketplace. These four key concepts became the foundational pillars upon which God would build our church in the days to come. They released hope, unity, diversity, miracles, discipleship, growth and community influence in our congregation. Here's a simple explanation of each:

SUBSTANCE

That night at the leadership conference, the Holy Spirit urged me to pursue "substance"—which I interpreted as the literal presence of God and the accurate testimony of Jesus. He was calling me to welcome genuine demonstrations of God's power that, truthfully, exceeded my own level of comfort.

To some that may not seem profound, but for me it was a course correction. I had fallen in love with church growth at the expense of the supernatural. I valued the comfort and safety of our guests more than I did God's presence. I had failed to understand that His presence brings hope to people, regardless of their religious backgrounds or spiritual condition. It was more pleasing to God to have a reputation for "substance" than to be known for the beauty and precision of our "safe" Sunday morning worship services. God was calling me to stop playing it safe!

COVENANT RELATIONSHIPS

That night the Holy Spirit also showed me the value of covenant relationships. Most relationships rely on contracts. As long as the parties honor the agreement, they remain friendly. These relationships tend to remain shallow, however, because they are based on the premise one of the parties will likely fail the partnership. God, on the other hand, offers covenant relationships. He lovingly commits to our well-being, fully anticipating there will be times we disappoint Him. Because of God's nature and unyielding love for us, He remains faithful even when we are not faithful to Him.

Covenant relationships within the church are liberating. If a person becomes destructive to himself or others, it gives believers permission to address the matter without fear of hurt feelings or retaliation. This level of unity translates into more signs and wonders. In the Book of Acts there are many references to the unity of believers: Early Christians were "in one place," "in one accord" and "of one heart and one soul." In each instance, the Holy Spirit was permitted to move among them powerfully.

Jesus prioritized successful relationships to the point that He instructed His followers to postpone praying or giving offerings until their relational conflicts were resolved (see Matthew 5:23,24). Christ commands us to value relationships just as God the Father, the Holy Spirit and Jesus himself support one another. Each personality within the Godhead lives to support, promote and celebrate the other. It's hard to imagine the Father saying, "Son, they're singing more songs about You than Me" or the Son saying, "I did all the groundwork; why do you get all the credit?" At Trinity Church we are learning, out of covenant relationships, to hold one another accountable and celebrate each other's victories.

LEGACY

The Holy Spirit also revealed to me the importance of establishing a legacy that future generations can emulate. "Legacy" denotes the belief that the coming generations have potential for both good and evil. Having an emphasis on that legacy helps us focus on equipping children and grandchildren to build upon the foundation the parents started. Practically, it places a priority on including children and youth in the activities of a church and family, fully anticipating that the next generation could achieve more than the one that precedes it.

MARKETPLACE

When the Holy Spirit spoke the word "marketplace," I wasn't exactly sure what He had in mind. But it soon became clear He wanted to rearrange my ministry values by measuring the success of our church by what happens outside its walls, not just in church services. Consequently we implemented a strategy to equip marketplace ministers, exhorting them to strategically recognize their workplace as a venue from which to offer hope to people in search of purpose and healing.

In addition, our church became more deliberate in being organically connected to the heartbeat of the city. We assumed more responsibility for the spiritual climate of Cedar Hill. We initiated citywide prayer efforts, participated in community events, influenced government and school board decisions, supported businesses and civic organizations, mobilized volunteers, reached out with compassion to families in need and young unwed mothers seeking direction and offered assistance to our community leaders.

We wanted to ensure that our community saw our church as a force for action rather than just a large, impersonal building where people congregated once a week for an event. We wanted to be known more by our deeds than our billboards.

At Trinity Church these four core values became our "menu of hope" for people in the community. Without hesitation, we began promising them an encounter with God (Substance); lasting friendships (Covenant Relationships); a place where their children would be treasured (Legacy); and a network that would help them excel for God at work (Marketplace).

Those four words, or concepts, lifted me from my spiritual funk and transformed the ministry of Trinity Church. If you are in a spiritual rut and you can't seem to crawl your way out, ask the Holy Spirit to lower a rescue rope. Ask Him to give you a word that will renew your purpose and give you a fresh vision.

In the time of Nehemiah, Jerusalem was a heap of rubble. Its walls had been destroyed, and the enemies of the Jews were celebrating the defeat of God's people. Yet in that dark time, the Bible says God gave Nehemiah not only a holy burden for the ruined city but a strategy to rebuild it. After he supernaturally received the funding for this project from a Gentile king, he journeyed back to Israel to begin the most ambitious renovation project in history.

Nehemiah found the grace to carry out this endeavor as God gave him a divine plan. God gave me a similar plan for our church—and He will do the same for you, regardless of the rubble you see piled all around you. Expect Him to speak! And when He does, follow His strategy and you will experience an amazing victory.

QUESTIONS FOR DISCUSSION:

1. *What needs to happen for you to be lifted from your spiritual rut?*
2. *What circumstances in your life right now need to change?*
3. *Has God already begun to give you a plan to turn things around? List at least one step you know you must take to begin this process.*

10

> *When we set our sights on God's dreams for our lives, our current condition is colored by His promise of what is to come.*

GOD'S DREAMS FOR YOU

I love a good dream where you defeat a villain, come to someone's rescue, win a reward, ride in a ticker-tape parade or score a winning touchdown. But don't you hate it when you wake up and realize the dream wasn't real? Of course, if it was a nightmare you are grateful it was just a dream—like the time I dreamt that Beck tattooed herself to look like former NBA forward Dennis Rodman!

God loves to give His people dreams. When a drought threatened thousands of lives in Egypt, God gave Joseph a dream about saving the people. He gave Abraham a dream about a nation of kings and priests that would help the world find redemption. He sent a dream to Joseph that a Savior would be supernaturally born from the Virgin Mary. What dream is God sending you? He wants to fill you with vivid images of what He can do through your life.

In 1976, a group of eighteen spiritual pioneers had a God-given dream to plant Trinity Church in South Dallas County. Almost immediately the church experienced God's favor, and the congregation earned a sterling reputation in the community. But in the church's eighteenth year, when one of the pastors resigned due to allegations of an inappropriate relationship, the church was devastated. Nevertheless, against great odds, the founders believed God's purpose for Trinity Church would still come to fruition. They continued to pray for God's protection and purpose.

At times I feared their dream would die and that Trinity would be forced to close its doors. But a turning point came in 1996 when we needed an additional $60,000 to cover expenses. It might as well have been $6 million. We needed a miracle!

That miracle came on a Wednesday evening, when an unassuming woman visited our church service. She placed a check in the offering plate for $12,000. We tried to contact her to express our gratitude, but our phone calls weren't answered. Needless to say, we were delighted when she attended another service a week later. This time she gave a check for $18,000, but she slipped out before I could say thank you.

I asked a staff member to pay this woman a visit the following week. I was bewildered to learn, however, that the address on her check didn't exist. When she attended the third Wednesday night service, and gave an additional $26,000, we were cautiously elated. We wanted to believe God had met our financial need through this "mystery woman," but we were also filled with uncertainty when the bank informed us that no such checking account existed. We couldn't understand why the other two checks hadn't bounced. We also braced ourselves, anticipating that the third check wasn't legitimate. To our surprise, that check was also funded. We would never see the mystery woman again.

Through this experience, God sent us a message that His dream for Trinity Church was still alive. The dream may have been temporarily buried under the rubble of human failure, but God was still working to build something beautiful.

DEALING WITH UNCERTAINTY

My grandmother is more than ninety years old. She's gone through two world wars, the Great Depression and all the current global upheaval we've experienced since the 9/11 terrorist attacks. She knows hardship. And, because she has seen God intervene time and again, she has great faith that He will sustain us in these perilous times.

Most of us younger people, until recently, have only known prosperity and opportunity. But uncertainty has now returned to our nation with the rise of militant Islam, the banking crisis, school shootings, global epidemics and horrific natural disasters. Despite ominous conditions in the world today, we do not have to dread the future. We can rest on the promise that God has a dream for our lives and our local churches.

How we view the future determines the way we live. As an employee, you will tend to have a better work ethic and be more patient, hospitable and persevering if you keep your eyes on the reward of our labor—your paycheck and the satisfaction of completing a job. Similarly, when we set our sights on God's dreams for our lives, our current condition is colored by His promise of what is to come. In other words, we find peace and comfort by keeping one eye on the present and another on the future.

God's dream for the present is that His believers would worship together in covenant relationship, promote the testimony of Jesus, infiltrate the marketplace, reach many people with the gospel and leave a legacy of genuine goodness to the next generation. His dream for the future is that we would reside with Him in heaven—free from uncertainty and free for eternity.

The lyrics of a popular children's nursery rhyme contain an important message for the church today: "When we all pull together, together, together … how happy we'll be." Although "happy" certainly understates the promise of God, the message is clear: It's better for believers to be together than to be apart.

When a friend is facing a crisis, we know what to do: On their behalf, we pull together in prayer and petition a transcendent God, knowing that nothing will interfere with His plans and dreams for that person's life. Regardless of a person's conditions or circumstances, God doesn't want us to give up on His dreams for our friends. We demonstrate our confidence in His love, power and dreams by pulling together in prayer.

One day I received an inspiring letter from a couple attending our church. Their twenty-two-year-old daughter had been killed in a motorcycle accident, leaving them responsible for raising two grandchildren. Despite their grief, they wrote about their hopes for the future and expressed gratitude for the prayerful support of their church family. With the help of believers, they could claim God's promise of hope.

A young man named Jesse was only thirteen when his organs began to shut down and his heart rate dropped. Doctors said they were doing all they could. Jesse's parents and friends gathered around his bed and prayed. They believed God still had a plan for Jesse's life. Almost immediately the boy began to regain strength and his organs began to function. Today Jesse is leading a healthy, productive life.

John, Aric, and Ariel were each involved in serious automobile accidents. In each case, doctors diagnosed brain damage and gave them little chance of recovery. But my daughter Katee and other young people remained at the hospital for days, pleading with God to spare their lives. In each instance, these young people miraculously recovered.

We can't underestimate the power of prayer and the impact God's dreams can have on our lives.

REJOICE ANYWAY!

During his second missionary journey, the apostle Paul was supernaturally directed to the region of Macedonia, in northern Greece. The Book of Acts tells us that he had a vision of a Macedonian man who was calling to him and saying, "Come over to Macedonia and help us" (Acts 16:9). This instance of divine guidance led Paul and his team to Philippi, a Greek city that was deeply infected with occultism and pagan philosophies.

After Paul cast out the occult demon that possessed a slave girl, he and Silas were thrown in jail. You can visit this site today. The "inner dungeon" of the jail, where the two missionaries were held in stocks, also served as the sewer for the city. So you can imagine what it would have been like to stay in this place. It was dark and dank—and it smelled horrible!

Yet the Bible tells us that after Paul and Silas began to sing and praise God, an earthquake suddenly shook the place, all the doors opened and everyone's chains fell off (Acts 16:25,26). Paul then stopped the Philippian jailer from committing suicide and led the man and his family to faith in Jesus. A vibrant church was later established in Philippi.

Eleven years after this incident, while Paul was composing a letter to the Philippians from another jail cell in Rome, he wrote these famous words: "Rejoice in the Lord always; again I will say, rejoice" (Philippians 4:4). In fact, the word "joy" or "rejoice" appears in various forms sixteen times in the Book of Philippians.

How can a letter about joy be written from a prison cell? How could the apostle Paul sing praises to God in the midst of rusty chains and sewage? Most of us don't get happy until circumstances make us happy. Yet Paul had a supernatural joy that was not based on circumstances. In fact, his joy actually changed the circumstances!

When Paul wrote Philippians, he probably remembered his time in the dungeon in Philippi. And in his

Roman cell he faced possible execution. Yet he did not wallow in self-pity or talk about himself or his problems. His focus was always on others. He said to the Philippians: "I thank my God in all my remembrance of you" (Philippians 1:3). In verse seven he said: "For it is only right for me to feel this way about you all, because I have you in my heart." In verse eight he tells the Philippians that he longs for them "with the affection of Christ Jesus."

This shows me that Paul's faith, love and joy were authentic. They were not pretend. He didn't have joy because everything was going his way. His love for his converts wasn't conditional. Even in the worst circumstances, the essence of genuine Christianity oozed out of the apostle Paul. He knew nothing of cotton candy religion.

This also shows me that Paul was able to hold onto his dreams no matter what was happening around him. Despite riots, setbacks, prison cells, beatings and shipwrecks, Paul kept believing and continued rejoicing. His love did not shift with the winds of change. His dream of spreading the message of Christ to the entire Roman Empire was not snuffed out, regardless of how many months he stayed in chains. His passionate faith kept burning.

GOD HAS AN ALTERNATE ENDING

Today some movies on DVD offer alternate endings. If viewers don't care for the original script, they can select another ending that is more to their liking. Many of us also need to be prepared for alternate endings. God has planned something better than you first imagined! Predictions of your spiritual demise (or your church's irrelevance) are premature. God still has dreams for your life, your family and your local church. He just doesn't want you living on cotton candy when He has so much more to offer.

I am challenging you to break your addiction to the type of stale religion that fails to satisfy your spiritual hunger. Take your eyes off spiritual leaders and religious organizations that are businesses masquerading as ministries. Then simply pursue the pure, unadulterated love of your Heavenly Father. Let His love become your ambition by practicing your faith and asking God to reveal His dreams for your life.

In John 17, Jesus prayed for you. Specifically He prayed that you would reach your potential. He prayed that His own potential would find its way into the hearts and minds of His children. So, it's fair to say, He doesn't want you settling for cotton candy religion that dissolves into nothing. That's not the happy ending He has planned for you. His dream for you promises to energize your life with His power and presence.

You can surrender your life to God's dream by reciting this prayer right now:

God, I come today to receive Your dream.
I believe You want good things for my life,
my church, my community and my nation.
Open my mind to the ideas and plans
that unveil Your glory through me.
Nothing from You will seem too small or
too big. Don't let me miss my alternate
ending. I give myself to pursue Your
intentions for my life.
Amen.

QUESTIONS FOR DISCUSSION:

1. *Describe a time when God miraculously pulled you out of difficult circumstances.*

2. *Are you wrestling with guilt or regret over something in your past that is preventing you from receiving what God has for you today?*

3. *God has a better "ending" for your life than you have imagined. Can you describe an "alternate ending" to your situation that would be the answer to your prayer?*

TO CONTACT THE AUTHOR

Jim Hennesy
pastor@trinitychurch.org

or
for bulk orders

Trinity Church of Cedar Hill
1231 E. Pleasant Run
Cedar Hill, TX 75104
(972) 291-2501

www.trinityministries.org